# 3rd edition

# PC Music

## the easy guide

Robin Vincent

PC Publishing

PC Publishing
Keeper's House
Merton
Thetford
Norfolk IP25 6QH
UK

Tel +44 (0)1953 889900
Fax +44 (0)1953 889901
email info@pc-publishing.com
website http://www.pc-publishing.com

First published 2006

© PC Publishing

ISBN 1 870775 201

British Library Cataloguing in Publication Data
A catalogue record for this book is available from the British Library

Cover design by Hilary Norman Design Ltd

Printed and bound in Great Britain by Biddles, Kings Lynn, Norfolk

# Contents

# Introduction

C omputers. Damn them and the evil that resides in their circuits! The intrusion, the aggravation, the childlike demand for attention, the incessant whirring and blinking of lights, the way they draw you in with promised delights, feign friendly intelligence and then unexpectedly turn on you just when you think you've got the hang of it, or more usually when you are about to show you wife/husband/dog something clever. A curse we've grown accustomed to. You may have bought one with the belief that it'll help you do the accounts, or write letters, help your kids with their homework or maybe let you print your own flyers for your next gig. The reality can often be one of miscomprehension, feelings of inadequacy and even fear. However, the last couple of years have seen normal people, everyday people, start to tug the computer out of the grasp of the nerdy, geek, pasty-faced computer user and are discovering the excitement, joy and wonder of what this technology can really offer. You get a digital camera for Christmas, you plug it into the computer and suddenly you're looking at pictures on screen. This leads you to working out your email so you can send your pictures to your friends and family. Email leads to links to the World Wide Web with vast storehouses of information, entertainment and badly disguised rubbish. Printers and scanners are purchased, online music discovered, speakers attached, DVDs viewed and very soon you're a MSM Messaging, Photoshop tweaking, Napster listening, Internet navigating, computer conquering wizard!

It's almost ten years since I began writing the original version of this book and I can tell you that the computer world is a much nicer place these days. You may not have quite got there yet but the general fog and mystery surrounding computers is fading and the way we look at the machine is changing. What I would like to do is to dig even deeper, to peel back more layers of beige, and show you the hidden potential that sleeps within the bleeping, whirring box sitting under your desk. With a little bit of software, maybe some carefully chosen hardware and enough knowledge to make you dangerous I hope to demonstrate how a computer can become an all singing, all dancing, bona fide, recording studio (and so much more).

My computer, the one on which I'm writing this book, is nothing extraordinary, a couple of years old, although quite up to date and powerful at the time, and yet it's a recording studio, a mixing and editing suite, a multi-effects processor, an instrument with a huge library of sounds, a sampler, a drum machine, an arranger, a compositional tool, score writer, mastering facility, CD duplicator and publishing/distribution house – oh, and I write letters, do my accounts, use email and even play games. It is truly a thing of wonder and requires no more knowledge or grasp of technology than that required to use an effects pedal or a tape recorder. Don't be fooled into thinking that computers only do electronic dance music, that's like saying Microsoft Word only lets you write non-fiction. I'm a musician, a guitarist, used to call myself a singer/songwriter, hatching out tunes on my four-track, until about ten years ago when I got hold of my first piece of multi-track recording software. It was very simple, four tracks of audio and MIDI. I wired up my guitar to the microphone socket on my soundcard (not ideal but it worked) and recorded a few chords. Then I chose another track and recorded some riffs along side – so far so four-track. What happened next changed my life. I'd recorded four bars of the same riff, I'm a terribly sloppy player so the first riff wasn't very good as I wasn't concentrating, the second one wasn't bad, the third was spot on and the fourth was nonsense. Using the mouse I was able to select the first two bars and the last one, cut them (like you would with a razor blade on tape) and delete them. Next I selected the third bar, the one I liked, and clicked 'Copy', moved the marker to the first bar and clicked 'Paste' – just like you would with text in a word processor. A couple more pastes and all four bars were playing back with that perfect third bar riff. With my four-track the mistakes in my playing would drive me to despair, the constant re-recording often meant losing all sense of what I was trying to create in the first place. What I realised is that with the computer I can sketch out the music in my head quickly and easily without losing my thread or feeling like a rubbish guitarist. I could take the best bits of my playing and my best ideas and cut away the bad stuff. I never touched my four-track again and I had only begun to scratch the surface.

The purpose of this book is to share the secrets of what your computer is capable of, to demonstrate what software and hardware you might need to make music and to look at how it all fits together. By the end of the book you should have a firm grasp of what's possible and confidence in what you need to make the music you want to make. I don't wish to dictate to you so I've used examples from as many different bits of software as I can, and once you understand the concepts of soundcards you'll be able to walk into any intimidating music shop and tell them exactly what you want.

# Acknowledgments

I would like to express my thanks to everyone who has bought this book over the years and especially to those who take the trouble to get in touch. Since it was first published in 1999 I've received a steady stream of emails from readers telling me how this book has helped them make sense of their computer music studios and ambitions. Being able to help people on this journey is what makes it all worthwhile.

I'd like to dedicate this book to my wife Maria for her unending love and support and also to baby Cloud (working title) whose forthcoming birth in December will herald the beginning of a whole new adventure.

# What can a PC do?

There are six main areas where a PC can contribute to your music making:

### MIDI sequencing
You may be familiar with this through the use of workstation keyboards or MIDI file players. It's the ability to record, edit and playback the keys pressed on a MIDI keyboard. On a computer you have complete mouse driven editing control over each note, each parameter. You can paint notes on screen and compose things that would be impossible to play (if you like).

### Scoring
MIDI data contains the same information as you'd find on a sheet of music. Your MIDI sequencer can often display the data as a score or with more specialised software you can create scores directly, to a professional, publishable level and hear them playback through software instruments.

### Software instruments
An enormous palette of sounds is available in software. From models of vintage synths like the MiniMoog and Prophet 5, through to the real instruments of the orchestra painstakingly sampled for breathtaking accuracy, and beyond into new forms of synthesis and sampling.

### Audio recording and editing
Slap a microphone in front of something and record live sound into your computer, Slice, cut, copy and paste on screen, where every detail of that sound is displayed giving you the best chance of creating the perfect sound and the perfect track. No real limit on the number of tracks you can record which gives you the freedom to explore your creativity.

### Mixing and effects
The quality of effects you can run on a computer now matches that of the hardware world, in fact some hardware companies also have software versions available. All the parameters on screen, all automatable alongside the tracks they are effecting. Mix hundreds of tracks together and use a huge variety of effects, EQ and dynamic processing to get the sound you want and often a sound you hadn't even thought of.

---

**Info**

Automation – the recording of fader or knob movements within a project so that all the changes are repeated in the playback. Almost all software parameters are automatable – for example, reverb depth, delay time, mix, level, pan etc.

## Mastering and publication

Mix down everything on the computer at the highest quality and resolution for CD or DVD. You can of course create your own audio CD's, even print the label, or create a master to send off for duplication. Alternatively the Internet provides a new way of releasing your music as an MP3 file. You can do all this on the same machine.

**Figure 1.1**
Steinberg's Cubase studio recording software with everything open.

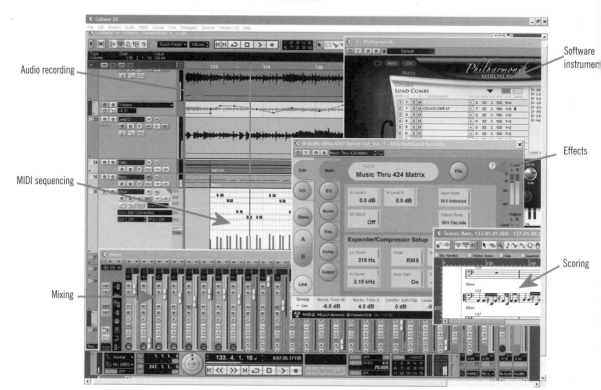

If that seems a bit overwhelming then let's take a few simple, practical examples:

### Singer/songwriter

It might be just you, guitar and a microphone, wanting to make some music. The computer gives you the ability to record multiple tracks and use the best bits, gives you guitar effects and amp modelling, and software drum machines and accompaniment – perfect.

### Electronic loop head

You want to make loops, create beats and thread them together with noises and beeps and sweeps and banging kick drums. On a computer you can trigger and arrange samples, loops, hits, and add vocal lines, live percussion, whatever you want. You don't have to study or understand music, you can just play with sound and develop creative, beat driven ideas.

### Composer

You're wanting to write for TV or film, or maybe the theatre, creating pieces of music for orchestra or groups of musicians. The computer can give you on-screen scoring, editing, arranging and instead of using just your piano you can call up a wide range of realistic software orchestral instruments to give you an idea about how it could really sound.

### Band

You and a bunch of mates, in a rehearsal room (unless you have under-standing/deaf neighbours) with lots of microphones and a laptop. You can plug everyone into the laptop, record multiple tracks and then take it home for mixing, where you can, if you want, change, alter, re-record, add synths, loops, noises etc.

### Dunno, just want to make some tunes

You may have no idea what you really want to do or how to go about it, which is why you're reading this book! On the computer you can muck about with inexpensive software that'll help you bang out some tunes, develop your ideas and start you down the road to wherever you want to go. It really is a freeing and creative leisure pursuit.

Whatever sort of music, whatever format, and whatever you want to achieve, the tools are there to help you do it. The best question you can ask is 'What do I want to do?' If you have even a half baked answer to that then it's a start.

## MIDI and audio

It's important to understand the differences between these two facets of computer music. MIDI sequencing and audio recording are both tied up in the same software and doing very similar things. However, what they are and how they are treated is very different. The problem is that misunderstanding leads people to make wrong decisions, wrong assumptions about what is and is not possible and generally end up struggling with the whole music making deal. The lines between the two can get very blurred, often in a good way, so let's look at both in some detail and try to give you a solid grasp of what we're talking about.

### MIDI

MIDI stands for Musical Instrument Digital Interface, and is essentially a com-puter language which allows different MIDI devices to 'talk' to each other. MIDI is a stream of instructions sent from one MIDI device to another in order to produce a response. MIDI instructions include 'note on', which contains information telling a MIDI device to play a note of a certain pitch at a certain 'velocity' or loudness, 'pitch bend' which tells the device to apply a bend in pitch to the sound currently being made, and 'program change' which tells the device to choose another sound. There are also 128 different 'controllers' available in MIDI, which have many different uses; they could control the faders on a MIDI mixing desk, the depth of effect on a MIDI effects unit, or even the movement of lights on a MIDI lighting rig.

Probably the simplest use of MIDI is to connect the 'MIDI OUT' of a keyboard to the 'MIDI IN' of a sound module. Striking a key on the keyboard sends instructions for that 'event' down the cable to the sound module, which responds by playing a sound. The keyboard itself hasn't made any sound, it has just sent an instruction to a MIDI device that responds to that instruction by generating a sound. This in itself is marvellous (!), but the best thing about MIDI is that the information sent between MIDI devices can be recorded, stored and edited by a MIDI sequencer. A 'sequencer' used to be a piece of hardware that could store a sequence of notes and play them back on request. Modern software sequencers can do far more than their name implies, but the essence is still the same. When you play your MIDI keyboard into your sequencing software, all the information on what notes were pressed, how hard etc, is being recorded as MIDI data. No sound is being recorded, just information on how the music was played.

A good analogy would be that of a sheet of manuscript paper. Written music contains no sound of its own, it simply conveys information on how that music should be played. A MIDI sequencer holds exactly the same information and can often let you create and print out the score using the recorded MIDI data. To hear the music written (or recorded) on the manuscript you would give it to a musician who would then be able to play it back on their instrument for you. Similarly In order for a MIDI sequence to create a sound on playback, the MIDI information must be routed to something that understands it and can play back sound in response.

**Figure 1.2**
MIDI contains the same sort of
information as sheet music

So, when recording MIDI, the sequencer does not record any sound at all, purely data. This has some considerable advantages over audio recording. Since only data has been recorded, then it can be changed or edited very easily. Continuing the sheet music analogy; to edit a piece of sheet music, you can simply erase existing notes and add new ones with a pencil, and then ask your musician to play it again – you could also ask your musician to use a different instrument this time. None of this would be possible if the original performance of the music had been recorded through a microphone as audio, but with MIDI, we can change every aspect of that information (what notes were played and when etc.), and then edit the playback sound, or even change it for a completely different instrument.

### Audio

This is about the recording of sound, stuff we can hear, real live audio. Get a microphone and place it in front of something making a sound, plug that microphone into a recorder of some kind (you know, a cassette recorder or tape recorder) and you'll be able to record that sound and then rewind and play the same sound back afterwards. In essence this is what your computer can do but instead of tape you're using a hard disk. It is often called 'hard disk recording' or 'digital recording' or even 'audio sequencing', and all of these terms are correct in their own way.

**Figure 1.3**
The Neumann TLM103 microphone

A computer, provided that it has the correct equipment attached, can record sound. You could picture the computer as an open reel tape recorder, or a portable multitracker, or a cassette recorder, or any other recording device that you are familiar with, except that a computer records digitally to hard disk, and can do so much more with the recorded material than was ever possible with tape. Technology has now advanced to the stage where a single piece of recording software can provide all the mixing facilities and effects processing on recorded audio that was previously available only as a collection of expensive studio hardware.

The confusion between MIDI and audio arises because both are concerned with sound – MIDI generates sound and audio is sound, but how they are treated during the creation of music is completely different. The confusion is further exacerbated by the software; as a single piece of recording software can contain both, closely integrated, into one complete package. So if you are using software instruments, these are MIDI and so are sequenced, but their output is audio which appears on the software mixer alongside live audio tracks and can be treated in the same way. However, if you are using an external MIDI sound module then sound comes out of that module – not the computer – and it's this that causes all the trouble.

As we look through all these areas in greater detail over the coming chapters then the whole MIDI/Audio issue should become clear and, hopefully, obvious.

# Soundcards

C ommon computer music question: 'Where do I plug in my guitar?' Turning your humble computer into a kick ass studio falls at the first hurdle if it doesn't have something into which you can plug a jack cable. If you want to record live sound into your computer then you'll need to consider getting hold of the right soundcard. More than that though, even if you don't want to record live music, the quality of your output should be of concern to you as it affects your ability to hear and mix properly. Furthermore, are your soundcard's drivers up to the job? Let's see shall we?

Most computers come with a soundcard of some sort. If your computer has speakers and makes bleeps and noises then you have a soundcard. The majority of soundcards are designed for games, multimedia and playing CD/DVDs so not a lot of thought has gone into the idea of serious studio recording. Netherthertheless it is a place to start and we'll come onto the proper gear in a minute.

Let's look at the conventional soundcard. On the back of your computer you should find a row of coloured minijack sockets, these may be built into the motherboard next to the printer port or may be on a separate card in the slots to the right.

**Figure 2.1**
Sound Blaster Live, the traditional
'soundcard'.

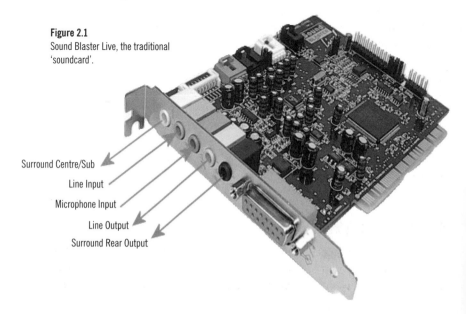

Surround Centre/Sub
Line Input
Microphone Input
Line Output
Surround Rear Output

Figure 2.1 shows a Creative Labs Sound Blaster Live card, a classic sound-card in the traditional sense. This is where the name 'soundcard' came from in that it's a card that slots into a motherboard and provides the computer with a sound system. The sort of soundcards we'll be talking about rarely come in this format these days but the name has remained. A colour coding convention of the soundcard inputs and outputs has developed which makes things a bit easier, but if in doubt you need to check your soundcard's doc-umentation, or you could just plug things in and out in a trial-and-error fash-ion and see what happens. Now I know the sockets are minijacks but you could take your guitar lead, put on an adapter and plug it into the pink micro-phone socket. A slightly better solution would be to come out of a preamp, or effects box and go stereo into the blue line input – this would give a rea-sonable input into the computer ready for recording. Would you expect the recording to sound any good? Well, if you think about it, you probably spent somewhere between £500 and £1000 on the computer, probably the same on your guitar, and yet your music making hopes and dreams all rest on a minijack socket on a soundcard that probably came included in your system for free. The built in soundcard is a starting point but it's also a long way from where we want to be. We want something designed for the job, that has the right connections, studio quality sound and rugged enough to be used when drunk.

**Figure 2.2**
Presonus Firepod

Here's something designed for the job:

The Firepod sports eight discrete mic preamps on the front, two of which can be instrument inputs all in a tasty 1U rack box. The quality is fabulous with 24bit and up to 96kHz recording. You've got mix and monitor outputs, S/PDIF and MIDI. You could record a whole band with this box.  Not quite enough inputs for you? Then how about buying two and daisy chaining them together giving you 16 microphone inputs over Firewire. At around £500 it's really not that expensive. Ok so this is probably over the top for most peo-ple but it gives you a clear idea of what we're talking about.

So a soundcard is a device, sometimes a card, more often an external box, that connects to the computer and allows you to record sound onto the hard disk and play back out again. What goes on inside a soundcard is a bit com-plicated so I'll try to explain it for you. Understanding the technology behind soundcards will allow you to make better choices and have a grasp of how the sound quality is affected – it's not essential stuff, but really very useful.

## Soundcard technology

The soundcard contains two integrated circuits, or chips if you like. One con-verts the incoming electrical or analogue signal from the mic etc. into digital information that can be understood and stored by the PC. This is called an analogue-to-digital converter (ADC). The other circuit does the complete opposite. It converts the digital information generated by the PC playing back the digital audio, back into an analogue signal that loudspeakers understand and therefore reproduces the sound. This is called a digital-to-analogue converter (DAC). So, digital audio is simply audio which has been through an ADC and is now 'digitised'. The quality of the converters has a direct effect on the sound quality of what you're recording in the same way that something recorded on a cheap and nasty tape recorder won't sound as good as something recorded on an expensive flashy tape machine. The converters on most soundcards are of the cheap and nasty variety, but hey, you have to start somewhere.

## Sampling and the dispute over digital quality

The process of A-to-D conversion is called 'sampling'. Now, this term is often misunderstood because of its association with samplers. A sampler does the same thing as a soundcard, in that it digitally records audio but it stores it in RAM (random access memory) and triggers the sound for playback via MIDI. It uses the recorded audio as a MIDI instrument in the same way as playing a piano sound on a synth. A PC samples audio and records it onto the hard-disk where it can be played back like a tape machine. It's a small difference but an essential one. To act like a sampler a PC needs additional software that uses system RAM and/or the hard disk to store samples for triggering.

Anyway, there are two factors involved in sampling; 'sampling rate' and 'resolution'. Sampling rate is measured in hertz (Hz) and denotes the number of times per second that the analogue signal is looked at (or 'sampled'). Resolution or bit rate is the number of values available to represent that signal, and is measured in bits. This is most easily explained in Figure 2.3.

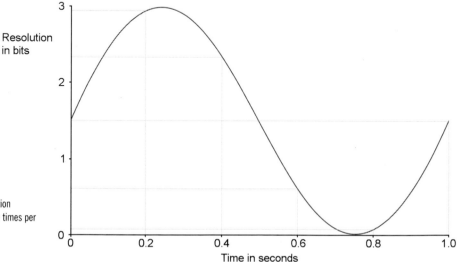

**Figure 2.3**
Audio signal of 1 second duration sampled at a rate of 5 Hz (five times per second).

Er... no it isn't, let me expand. The curve is an audio signal of one second in length. The sample rate is 5Hz because a measurement is being taken five times during one second. The resolution is 2 bit. The bit is a binary format so one bit would be 2 to the power of 1, two bit would be 2 to the power of 2, three bit 2 to the power of 3 and so on. So 2 bit, or two squared, gives the possibility of 4 (0 to 3) values. Computers can only deal with whole values represented by the 1's and 0's of binary.

So, at 0.2 seconds the signal is measured and is given a value of 3 because that is the nearest whole value. At 0.4 seconds the signal is given a value of 2, at 0.6 it's 1, at 0.8 it's 0, and 1.0 it's 2. The result shown in Figure 2.4 is the computer's representation of that audio signal.

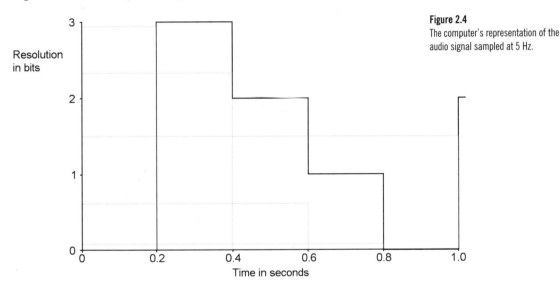

**Figure 2.4**
The computer's representation of the audio signal sampled at 5 Hz.

Close but no cigar. Well the conversion was pretty rubbish and on playback it would sound a lot like noise rather than the nice sine wave that went in. This is because the sample rate and resolution were pitifully low and only useful as an aid to understanding the concept.

## Digital 'quality'

When Sony and Philips invented the CD back in the early '80s they decided that 16 bit and 44.1kHz was what was required to perfectly replicate sound – that's a bit rate of 65536 (2 to the power of 16) possible values measured at 44,100 times a second - this has become known as 'CD Quality'. 16 bits were decided upon because it was probably the best that current technology could manage at the time and it seemed to do the job. The sample rate was based upon the Nyquist theorem. Dr Nyquist (sounds like a Bond villain to me) stated that, as all sound is made up from sine waves, and any sine wave can be created mathematically from knowing two values on the curve, then any sound can be accurately sampled using a sample rate twice that of the sound's frequency. So a pitch of 10kHz would need a sample rate of 20kHz to sample it with 100% accuracy. Human hearing goes up to about 20kHz (on a good day) and so in order to reproduce everything we can hear with you would need a sample rate of 40kHz. 44.1kHz was chosen to add a little bit of ballast as science is never quite so perfect in reality. The problem is that many people feel that a sampling rate of 96kHz just 'sounds better'. They claim that frequencies outside our hearing have an influence on the ones we can hear. The other issue is that of 'error correction'. As I mentioned before, computers can only deal in whole numbers and so each time a value is rounded up it loses accuracy. The more a piece of audio is processed the more inaccuracy creeps in until it becomes noticeable in the deterioration of the sound – increasing the sample rate and bit rate can improve this. Two other factors, 'headroom' and 'dynamic range' are affected by the bit rate and these need consideration. Headroom is the amount of level between the ideal and distortion. Dynamic range is the difference between the quietest and loudest sound. Bit rate is essentially a measurement of amplitude, or level. If your target product is a CD then you want to end up with a 16 bit recording. If you record using a 16 bit system then in order to get the benefit of all 16 bits you will have to record at the highest possible volume before distortion. The problem is that very few recordable sounds are at a constant level; take the voice for instance. If you set the optimum recording level bang on 16 bits any slight increase from the singer will result in distortion. To introduce more headroom you would reduce the recording level a touch so that only the loudest peak sounds fill all 16 bits. This means that the majority of the recording will probably be using maybe 12 or 14 bits.

One way of looking at it would be to see bits in terms of an LED meter in your recording software, or even on a mixer or hi-fi. If you were to attempt the same recording on a 24 bit system then you have effectively added a further 8 LED's onto the top of your meter, giving you loads of headroom. You could set your optimum recording level at the 20 bit mark and be completely confident that you will always fill the first 16 bits, making full use of CD quality. This is what also gives us our increased dynamic range. The distance between the possible loudest and quietest sounds has been increased giving a more 'dynamic' recording. Once the recording has been made you can 'dither' it back to 16 bit.

In any case the DVD Audio standard has become 24bit at 96kHz to take advantage of the perceived quality gains. There is also a file size issue, in that DVD quality takes up three times the amount of space that CD Quality uses, 30MB per stereo minute compared to 10MB (roughly), and of course DVD Audio will be in six channel surround which is 90MB per minute, and that much more data means the computer is working much harder to process it. At the end of the day I don't have a posh enough music system to hear the difference, however, I've found that working with 24bit audio files gives me a better quality 16bit file at mixdown than working with 16bit in the first place.

The final contributing factor is the quality of the soundcard in the first place, not quality in terms of bit and sample rate numbers but quality in terms of the physical technology, the chips and circuitry being used. Not all soundcards are the same, and there's a reason why professional studios spend large amounts of money on their gear. Cheap soundcards with cheap

## Dithering

Dithering is a process of intelligently reducing the bit rate of a recorded file. It would first remove the unused bits, like the top few, and also remove the bottom few that were always filled, and re-process the remainder. So, recording in 24 bit can ensure that you get the best possible quality out of 16 bit. It's also true to say that because 24 bit offers more values than 16 bit, then the recording, to most people, sounds clearer and even more accurate than 16 bit.

converters create noise. There can be noise inherent in the circuitry, noise created by the error correction and noise picked up by the card from the inside of the PC. Listen to your soundcard playing back an audio file and you'll probably hear a load of hiss as well. A card with a high signal-to-noise ratio can lower the noise interference, when recording, to almost nothing at all. Although, if a sound is recorded at a low resolution, it will play back at the same quality regardless of which soundcard you put it through. That said, sound quality is a very subjective and relative thing, and if it sounds good to you then go with it.

## Digital ins and outs

One way to bypass all this mucking about with the soundcard's analogue to digital conversion is to get hold of a soundcard with a digital input and output and do the conversion elsewhere. Now, a digital interface allows you to record audio onto your PC from another digital device such as a digital mixer. What does all that mean? Let me explain. Digital information (could be digital audio, could be software, could be just a file) can be moved between different digital devices and arrive in the new device in exactly the same state as when it left. Consider a floppy disk, CD or thumb drive. You can copy a file onto a floppy and put it into another PC and the file is exactly the same. That's because it's digital and it's remained in the digital domain throughout the transfer process.  So if you use a digital mixer, it will have very high quality converters and converts any incoming analogue audio into digital audio and you'll be able to take it direct to the computer via the digital interface. This way the quality of your soundcard is neither here nor there, it's just acting as an interface for the digital audio.

### Digital formats
There are a few digital formats that it's worth being aware of:

### S/PDIF (Sony Philips Digital Interface)
The most common digital format found on DAT machines, minidisk players and many soundcards. It's stereo and comes in two flavours of physical connection - optical, using fibre optic cable, and coaxial using RCA phono. You can get a little converter box to convert between the two.

### AES/EBU  (Audio Engineering Society / European Broadcast Union)
Essentially the professional version of S/PDIF using XLR connectors.

### ADAT  (Alesis Digital Audio Tape)
Alesis created an 8 track tape based digital recorder many years ago which used S-VHS video tape as its recording medium. Alesis then created an optical digital format for transferring audio between ADATs. The ADAT 8 channel 'lightpipe' format remains a very popular format and can be used to connect digital mixers to computers with ADAT soundcards.

### TDIF  (Tascam Digital Interface)

Tascam's alternative to ADAT using Hi-8 tape in their DA38 and DA88 digital recorders. TDIF uses a 25pin D-Sub connector similar to a printer port and is also still used on soundcards and digital mixers.

## Drivers

If you needed another reason why you should think about investing in a more professional soundcard then I'd like to draw your attention to the drivers. A driver is a piece of software that provides communication between the computer and whatever device is plugged into it – in this case, the soundcard. For regular games and multimedia cards the drivers are written to be very tolerant and good in any situation, this means that they have large buffers and built in delays to give the computer plenty of time to understand and process the data. These delays are known as 'latency' and you're talking about anything from half a second upwards. When playing a game that's nothing but when playing guitar that's a lifetime. Soundcards designed for music have special drivers written for them that make them much faster, to the point where latency has ceased to be an issue. Anything under 10ms (milliseconds) is generally regarded as completely playable and to put some kind of perspective on it 3ms is like standing a yard away from your guitar amp.

There are three main driver types to be aware of:

### ASIO (Audio System In Out)

This was developed by Steinberg, the creators of the popular Cubase music production software and has become the standard low latency driver for audio applications.

### WDM (Windows Driver Model)

This is a much enhanced version of the Microsoft Multimedia Driver which can provide very low latencies with specific music applications like Cakewalk's Sonar studio recording software.

### GSIF  GigaSampler InterFace

This is a specialised driver for running Tascam's GigaStudio sampler software.

So, out of all that all you really need to know is that a soundcard is a piece of hardware that has the ability to digitally record and playback audio. Super.

## Connecting MIDI devices to the computer

We talked in Chapter 1 about the differences between MIDI and audio. Every MIDI device has an interface consisting of at least one, 5 pin circular socket, or 5 pin 'DIN'. A DIN used to be an audio connection and was very popular when MIDI was invented, so it was chosen as a good format. The pin connections inside the cables and sockets differ from the audio type so you must get MIDI cables and not old audio DIN cables to connect MIDI stuff together. Anyway, most MIDI devices have two sockets, one labelled MIDI IN to receive information, one labelled MIDI OUT to send. Some have a third labelled MIDI THRU, this routes whatever information is coming into the IN straight back out allowing you to chain several MIDI devices together

If you have a MIDI keyboard or sound module you may notice that the computer doesn't naturally have the necessary MIDI ports to make the connection with other MIDI devices. What we need to do then is provide the computer with a MIDI interface.

**Figure 2.5**
MIDI sockets.

**Figure 2.6**
MOTU MIDI Express MIDI Interface allows eight separate MIDI devices to be connected to your PC.

MIDI interfaces can be found built into many soundcards and so no additional hardware is required. The joystick port can be configured to act as a MIDI interface. Those clever people at Roland came up with a driver called the MPU-401 (catchy name), which is included with Windows, to make this happen. All you need is a special adapter cable and you have one MIDI IN and OUT. Many modern MIDI controller keyboards come with USB ports which can connect directly to a computer, making the interface connection. Failing all of that, or if you have a number of external sound modules or other MIDI devices to connect to the computer, then you will need an external MIDI interface. These are available from any music technology store and come with different numbers of ports, usually 1x1, 2x2 and the 8x8 for more serious amounts of gear. A MIDI port can send and receive MIDI over 16 MIDI channels. A MIDI device with one MIDI port can respond on 16 MIDI channels. By having more ports you can send 16 channels to separate MIDI devices independently. Interfaces with 8 MIDI ports gives a total of 128 separate MIDI channels, so you could have 128 instrument sounds being played from your sequencer, more than enough for most people. All the MIDI ports are accessed through the software sequencer described in the next chapter.

To sum up the connections, all you would need is a MIDI cable between your keyboard's MIDI OUT port to the computer's MIDI IN (provided by an interface – this could also be done via a USB port built into the keyboard). The computer could then receive all the information generated by playing the keyboard and trigger your software instruments, or record the information into a sequencer. Alternatively you could route that MIDI information out to an external MIDI device by connecting the MIDI OUT of the computer to the MIDI IN of the external MIDI device. So, you can plug your MIDI performance into a very expensive synthesiser or sampler and feel astonished at how good you sound.

A good point to make here is that the actual sound comes out of whatever MIDI device you plug your MIDI information into. If you are using a software synth on the computer then the sound will come out of the soundcard's output, along with any audio. If you are using an external MIDI device then the sound will come out of that device. Seems obvious but you have no idea how many people miss this completely. If you want to know what this looks like then check out Chapter 12 'PC Music Setups'.

But why don't you just record the keyboard live? Well, because MIDI can be manipulated and edited and programmed to do all sorts of things and can be recorded without the need to be able to play an instrument, and can sound like a whole orchestra without having to hire one. I'll go into the joys of MIDI sequencing in the next chapter, but a simple example would be that you play in a few bars of a song on a keyboard but you're a bit of a sloppy player so your timing is awful and you've played a couple of bum notes. As MIDI is just simple data you can tell the computer to put all the notes you played on an even beat, then simply delete the notes which were wrong. You initially played the song with a piano sound but now you think it would sound better as a trumpet, no problem, tell the computer to change the sound that's being used. This would be impossible to do if the performance was recorded live as audio.

# MIDI sequencing

M any years ago in the heady days of analogue synthesis, when people mucked about with voltage controlled oscillators, amplifiers and filters all strung together with a tangle of patch leads, some bright spark came up with the idea of applying a cyclic timing device to the voltage input. Voltage level controlled the frequency of the oscillators and, therefore, pitch, so by varying the voltage you could play different notes. With this new timing device you could set different voltages (and therefore pitch) and get the timer to trigger them in 'sequence'. These devices or 'sequencers' usually consisted of eight parts and can be heard all over early 1980's pop music. Depeche Mode, Yazoo, Human League, Gary Numan along with Kraftwerk, Vangelis and Jean-Michel Jarre are good examples, or not, depending on your taste.

As synthesisers went digital, control voltage gave way to MIDI, and analogue circuitry and potentiometers gave way to data and memory. Although the implementation of recording and playing back MIDI data far outstripped the capabilities of the old analogue sequencers, the name stuck, and the increasingly inaccurate 'sequencer' remains. The weird thing is that in more recent times the old analogue way of doing things has been rediscovered and celebrated for its simplicity and ease of use, so much so that many modern bits of software now include analogue style sequencing as part of the package.

The possibilities now available in a software MIDI sequencing package are far beyond simply stringing a sequence of notes together. It's become a full on programming language and can be used to manipulate an increasingly varied array of products and functions. In this chapter I hope to shed a little light on the simpler functions of a MIDI sequencer so that you'll get an idea of what you could do with one.

The basic concept of the modern MIDI sequencer is the ability to record, edit and play back MIDI data. Software sequencers, of which there are several brands, generally follow the same format and have very similar editing possibilities. So the following examples should be applicable to whatever sequencer you are using.

## The arrange window

Also known as the track, session or project window, the arrange window displays an overview of what has been recorded. It consists of a vertical list of tracks and a timebase display showing blocks of data that have been record-ed relative to time. The time base is usually shown in bars and beats but this can also be real time in seconds, frames and even samples. This is far easier to show rather than to describe (Figure 3.1).

**Figure 3.1**
The Arrange window in Steinberg's Cubase SX.

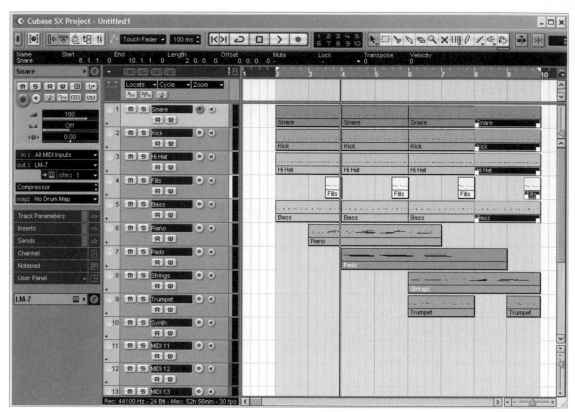

On the left hand side you can see a list of MIDI tracks. Each track has been given a name and on the far left there's a column that displays information on the allocated MIDI channel and what MIDI device the track is set to for output. Each track is playing a different instrument so each track has to be on a separate MIDI channel, with the exception of the four drum tracks at the top. The software drum kit I'm using is on a single MIDI channel but I have used different tracks to record the drums as I find it easier to edit each part separately. Similarly you could record two different piano parts on different tracks and allocate them the same MIDI channel because they are using the same instrument.

In the arrange window you can literally *arrange* your music. This is done by cutting up and moving the blocks of data around, or copying and pasting them. For instance, I only recorded two bars of the drum parts, I then copied and pasted them into the next two bars and so on (Figure 3.2).

The arrange window is also where you would usually do your recording. Providing you have a MIDI input device, like a keyboard, attached to your PC through a MIDI interface or USB port, and the MIDI inputs are enabled in the software, then you should be able to record straight into the program. Most sequencers have some sort of indicator showing MIDI activity. In the Cubase

Copy the first two bars

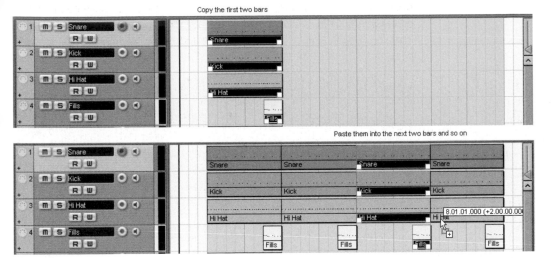

Paste them into the next two bars and so on

the transport bar has a MIDI IN and MIDI OUT LED which flashes when MIDI moves through the program. So if you hit the keys on your keyboard the lights should flash. If not then you may need to do a little more setting up before you can record anything.

So, to record a live MIDI performance here's what you do:

- Select a track for recording.
- Choose an output destination, or what synth and sound you want to use (this can always be changed later – because this is MIDI yes?).
- Set the tempo and turn on the metronome if you need it.
- Press record on the transport bar.
- Play with your entire soul.
- Press stop when you've finished.

**Figure 3.2**
Copy and paste – one of the wonders of software sequencing.

A block will have appeared alongside the track you were recording onto. Fantastic! You're now recording your own music, soon you'll be a star. Now let's copy and paste that block onto another track. If we give it a different MIDI channel we should be able to get the two tracks to play back together with different instrument sounds.

### How do you select the sound you want?

Each MIDI instrument has an address that consists of two numbers; Bank and Program (also called patch). The arrange page will give you a place where you can specify these numbers for each track. Consult the documentation of your MIDI device to find out which instruments these numbers refer to. If you have no other software instruments installed on your computer then you can use the 'Microsoft GS Wavetable SW Synth' that's included with Windows. This isn't a high quality software sound module designed for playing live from a keyboard, it's a General MIDI playback module for playing MIDI files. If you try to play it with a keyboard you'll encounter a huge latency of half a second or more. However, for playback it'll do if nothing else is available.

So far we've managed to record something and maybe you've even moved blocks of stuff around the screen but we haven't been able to actually edit any notes that we played. Also, if you don't play an instrument or you have no MIDI input device, then so far you've recorded nothing. Let's get into the first of a MIDI sequencer's editing pages to see what can be done about all that.

## Piano roll editor

This is also known as 'key edit', 'matrix editor', or just plain 'edit', but 'piano roll' is the most descriptively accurate term because that's what it looks like, a piano roll. What's a piano roll? Oh come on, it's a long roll of paper with holes punched in it to tell an old automatic piano what to play, like you see in old western movies. Anyway, a piano roll editor looks a bit like Figure 3.3 (it's from Cubase again because they claim to be the first people to have used it).

**Figure 3.3**
The piano roll editor.

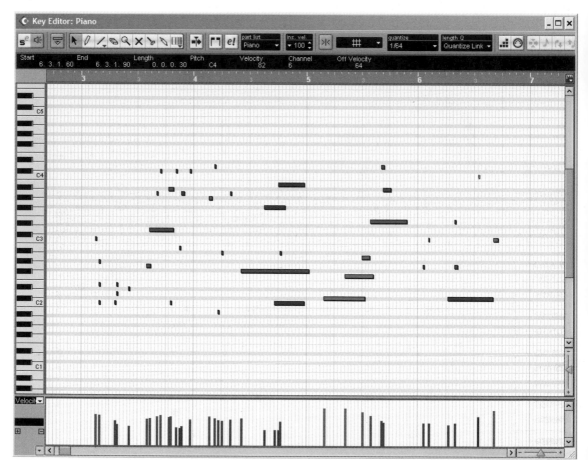

Down the left hand side you can see a representation of a piano keyboard. Along the top is the same timebase as found in the arrange page. In the main window lies a grid, the axis of which correspond to pitch and time. The dots shown represent the notes that have been recorded. The height of each dot denotes its pitch relative to the keyboard on the left. Its horizontal position shows its start point (when the note was struck) and its length shows how long the note was held.

So, you can easily see if you played a wrong note. You can then pick up the corresponding dot and move it to the correct position. You can copy and paste, and delete or whatever you want. You can also add notes using a pencil tool. So if you can't play a keyboard, this is where you can enter notes.

A handy variation of the piano roll editor has come about in the form of the drum grid editor. This is very similar but has a list of drum sounds down the left in place of the piano keyboard. The grid is usually tighter because note length isn't as important with percussive instruments. This has made drum programming far easier to cope with.

## MIDI controllers

The graphic editing of MIDI controllers makes adding events like pitch bend, modulation, volume and filtering an absolute doddle.

Controller editing is usually done in the piano roll window. This makes it easy to see which notes you are applying the control to.

In the example from Sonar (Figure 3.4), the bottom half of the window is showing the 'velocity' controller values. It refers to the starting velocity (how hard the note was struck) of each note. The velocity can be any one of 128 values (0-127), shown at the side. I have drawn in a rather obvious sort of fade in and out. You can see that the notes in the first two bars were hit with increasing velocity and in the second two bars the velocity gets softer. In the same way, I could draw in a pitch bend.

**Figure 3.4**
The piano roll in Sonar showing notes (top half) with velocity controller values (bottom half).

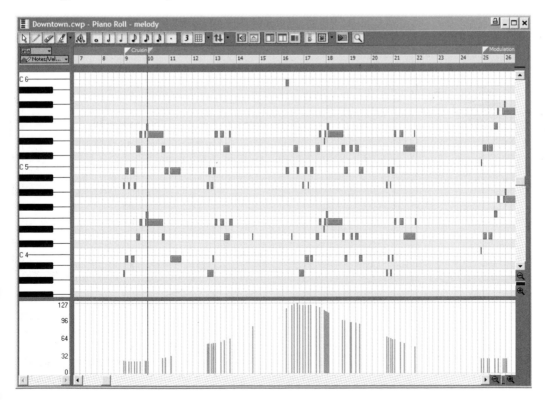

## Event list editor

Every time a piece of MIDI data is generated, by striking a key, moving the pitch wheel, or pushing a button etc. it is called a MIDI 'event'. A sequencer usually allows these events to be edited directly. This is a little hard-core for most people but it can be very handy for putting in controller data, patch changes and stuff, and it's also a good way of finding out what MIDI information is actually going on.

An event list simply lists all the MIDI events in time order. Figure 3.5 is part of the event list from a track in Cubase. It shows the information about each event, starting with the type of event, its start and end point, length and then data relevant to the event like note number or velocity.

**Figure 3.5**
The Event list editor in Cubase.

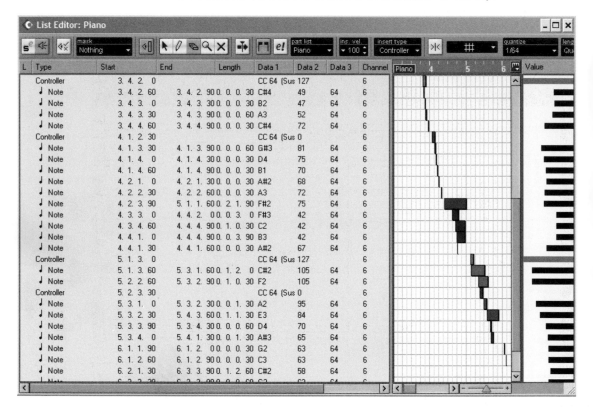

So, going through the list we can see that the first event is a controller with a controller number of CC64 – this is sustain. The sustain pedal was pressed just before the first notes were played and then the pedal was released a few notes later. Taking the first note you can see that it was in bar 3, beat 4 and was note C#4 played with a velocity of 49.

Any and every MIDI event will be listed here. They can be edited, added to and deleted. It's not a very musical part of sequencing but it can be useful for fine-tuning.

## Score editor

The information contained in a MIDI note event is mainly pitch and length. It's not very hard then to translate that information onto the musical stave. Most sequencers contain some form of score editing. Some just give you the option to print out the score, others allow you to edit notes directly on the stave, add dynamic markings, titles, lyrics, tablature and finally print out your score in a brilliantly desk-top-published kind of way. Most are somewhere in-between.

If you can read music then this could be a useful editing tool, otherwise it may be nice to have a printed score of your creation so that other people could play it. You can move notes about, add notes, delete, cut and paste, all the usual stuff, and print out.

**Figure 3.6**
Cubase's Score editor.

A dedicated notation package usually contains the best score writing tools. Some sequencers have excellent scoring facilities but rarely come up to the standard of the full-on, professional, scoring package – you'll find more about those in Chapter 7.

## Quantization

This is one of those terms that people like to use when they are pointing fingers and accusing music recorded on computers as being soulless, robotic or 'computerised'. In reality it's a really useful function that has enabled less than perfect musicians to produce music and has even spawned new musical genres. Quantization basically takes what you play and snaps it to a grid – you play along to a metronome as you're recording and if you are anything like me then your playing is all over the place. By quantizing you can automatically shift every note onto the beat. This is particularly useful when playing drums and percussion. Of course, if you want to keep the timing and expression you used when recording then don't quantize it, or only quantize those parts that were out of time. Quantization doesn't have to be rigid either, most sequencers have what we call 'Groove Quantize' where there's a certain amount of swing that can be used on the notes to give it a more human feel. It's also possible to create your own Quantize template or even extract a template from an audio drum loop so that everything you play stays in time with that loop.

Quantization is very clever and amazingly useful and you don't have to use it.

## MIDI effects and functions

As MIDI is really simple bits of data it's easy to apply a little bit of maths to it to do some cool things. For instance you can transpose an entire MIDI track just by entering how much you want to change it by. Another function could be to play a chord on a single note press. Specify the chord type and the sequencer does the rest. An arpeggiator is a really useful function found in synths that can just as easily be added at the sequencing stage. Most of these functions are dressed up as plug-ins which are inserted onto MIDI tracks. There are lots of interesting ways that MIDI can be manipulated beyond the recording of it into the sequencer.

MIDI sequencers are awfully powerful and offer a wealth of ways to record and edit MIDI data. Although it's getting on a bit and there have been better alternatives, MIDI has stood the test of time and continues to empower the likes of you and me to create, produce and arrange music.

# Hard disk recording

P reviously the toys of the rich and famous, the power of the PC has brought professional quality 'studio' recording to the home user for an increasingly affordable investment.

There are a few interchangeable terms here: hard disk recording package/program/system; audio sequencer; multitrack audio software. All of them mean the same thing - a computer based software system for recording onto hard disk.

Hard disk recording was initially a hardware thing. Chunky rack-mountable units with internal hard drives, designed to replace the analogue, open reel, tape based multitracker. This is still an easy and professional solution without all that mucking about with computers. However, computers were already involved in the recording process as sequencers and it wasn't long before they were connected to the hard disk recorders as control devices and editors. The problem at this stage was that the computer power couldn't really cope with the amount of data generated by recording and editing multiple tracks of audio. The audio inputs and outputs on computers were also rubbish (still are in many cases) and so, until technology brought them up to scratch, recording onto computers wasn't really a viable option.

In the mid 1990's, as the Apple Mac and Windows based IBM PC began to evolve, the possibilities of computer based sound recording started to emerge. By the time Windows 95 came along computer technology had advanced well beyond what was required to move digital audio through it's circuits. The professionals were focused on Digidesign, the creators of Pro Tools who were really the first to realise the potential of computer recording. They used dedicated hardware with external hard disks and custom made, high quality, inputs and outputs. This took most of the processing away from the computer in order to circumnavigate the limitations. The computers were used as the control centre and editing suite. Digidesign still produces the most professional software and hardware based recording systems.

So when do the rest of us get a look in? Well, what everyone wanted was a whole studio on their PC. Not just sequencing but also the ability to record real sound, vocal tracks, guitar tracks, and all for under the price of a decent four track tape based multitracker.

The sequencer software companies began to aim for this ideal and along with advances in processing power came integrated four track, then eight track systems using a computer's internal hard disk. The quality of sound-cards improved and some hardware manufacturers began producing sound-

**Figure 4.1**
Simply want a computer for recording?

cards expressly for audio recording. A fully working studio on a PC, for a few hundred quid, was only a matter of time. Programs like Cubase and Twelve Tone's Cakewalk surfed the front edge of the technology squeezing out amazing audio facilities that the professional world seemed to insist wasn't possible without serious investment in specialised hardware.

Today, it's here. In the last few years we have seen eight track audio soar to virtually unlimited tracks. Dynamics processing and real-time equalisation, the adding of real-time effects such as delay, chorus and reverb; hardware audio cards giving multiple ins and outputs with proper professional connectors, all for reasonable money. It's getting better and cheaper all the time.

### That's the history lesson, but what can you actually do with it?

Hard disk recording is about recording multiple tracks of audio onto hard disk - simple. Its concept is identical to that of tape. In a studio situation you record each instrument onto a separate track. Once recorded you can play the tracks back together and adjust the volume of each track until you get the correct 'mix' of sound. You can edit each track individually, add effects and other dynamic processing and also position, or pan, the track in the stereo or even surround sound field.

### So what does a recording studio on a PC contain?

Well, first thing you need is something to record onto, that'll be the hard disk. There will be a software mixing desk to allow you to alter levels. Effects (FX) boxes allowing you to add reverb and chorus etc. to individual tracks. Equalisation (EQ), these are like treble and bass controls on an amp, but on individual tracks. Some kind of sound or audio interface to allow for real inputs and outputs.

## Hard drives

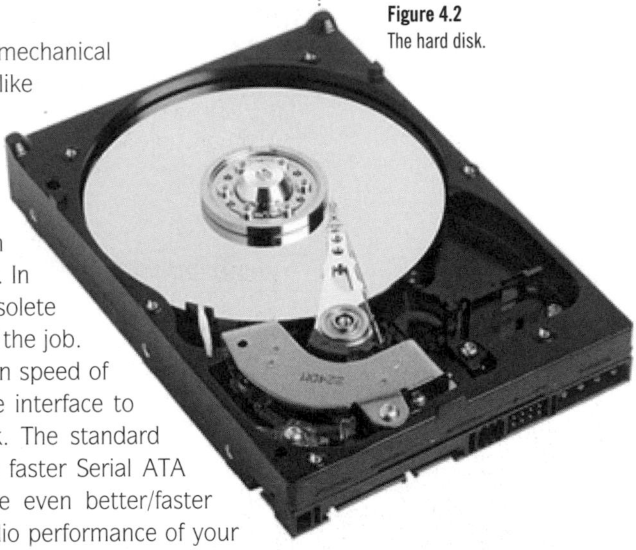

This is what we are recording to. They are a mechanical device with moving parts and specifications like spin speeds and access times which pretend to mean a lot to some people. A few years ago the type and speed of hard drive was really important. Professionals used SCSI (Small Computer Serial Interface) drives which had the superior speeds needed for audio work. In recent times SCSI has become more or less obsolete with regular hard drives being easily capable of the job. The standard internal hard drive will have a spin speed of 7200rpm, which is plenty and it's actually the interface to the motherboard that can cause a bottleneck. The standard Parallel ATA connection has given way to the faster Serial ATA connection meaning that newer systems have even better/faster drives – hooray! One way of improving the audio performance of your system is to use RAID (Redundant Array of Inexpensive Disks). This was designed for servers really but the technology is useful in that using RAID'0' we can combine two or more hard drives that are 'striped' into a single high performance drive. You can get about a 40% increase in track count, if you need it, the only proviso being that if one drive fails you loose all the data on both. Laptops generally come with smaller and slower 5400rpm hard drives. These are capable of about 60% of a regular desktop drive which is still rather good and you can get faster 2.5' laptop drives. There's also the option of external hard drives that can connect via USB or Firewire that will give laptops better audio performance.

**Figure 4.2**
The hard disk.

### Rough guide to hard drive track counts:

Recording at CD quality (16 bit 44.1kHz):

* Regular computer drive – 120 tracks of audio
* RAID0 drive – 200 tracks of audio
* Laptop drive – 80 tracks of audio

Recording at DVD quality (24bit 96kHz):

* Regular computer drive – 70 tracks of audio
* RAID0 drive – 120 tracks of audio
* Laptop drive – 40 tracks of audio

That's the basis of your studio. Digital recording also allows for all sorts of editing not really possible with tape, like copy and paste, normalisation and looping.

Let's have a look at the software. You can get dedicated hard disk recording software but the most popular ones are those which are integrated into a MIDI sequencer, and that's what I'll use as examples.

**Figure 4.3**
The Pro Tools 'Arrange', 'Project', or 'Session' window showing audio and MIDI tracks.

## The arrange window

Yep, this is exactly the same as the arrange window in a MIDI sequencer, but this time we have audio tracks recorded alongside MIDI tracks (Figure 4.3).

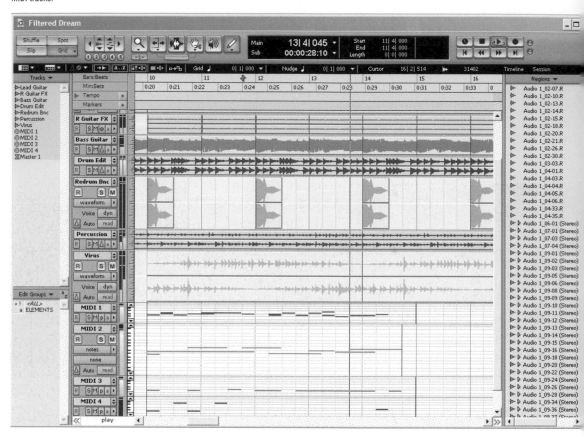

The layout should be familiar but now we can see several audio tracks in the arrange window as well as a couple of MIDI tracks. The audio tracks are visually represented by blocks, as the MIDI is, but you can see within these blocks what looks like a mess of 'stuff'. This is a graphical representation of amplitude (volume) over time of the audio track – like what you might have seen on an oscilloscope at school. This is how an audio file is usually portrayed.

The same editing rules apply in this page as they did to the MIDI blocks. You can copy and paste them and move them around, as long as they remain on an audio track, MIDI and audio are not interchangeable. You can see that the 'R Guitar' and 'Bass guitar' have had the same bar copied and pasted throughout that part of the project. So I can use the same riff over and over again without having to recod it more than once – handy.

You soon find that you don't actually have to play everything right all the time. If you record one or two takes of a guitar track you'll probably find that you have enough 'right' bits to make one good track. For example, you've got a complicated riff going through each verse but it's really hard to play. You record yourself playing the riff for a couple of minutes, pick out the one that sounded the best and paste it throughout the whole song. Hardly rock and roll but who's going to notice? Besides you can leave all that practising stuff for when you're booked to play Glastonbury.

The arrange window is also home to the display and editing of automation. Everything that can be done in the mixer can be automated but let's look at the mixer functions first and come back to this in a moment.

## The mixer

Okay, so where's this mixer you talked about?. Figure 4.4 shows Cubase's mixer in all its glory. It's got faders for track volume, panning controls, 'sends' for routing out to busses, 'inserts' for effects, EQ with either knobs or a curve display, whopping great big and colourful meters, in fact everything an analogue desk has and a lot more.

**Figure 4.4**
Cubase's mixer with various display options open in the top half.

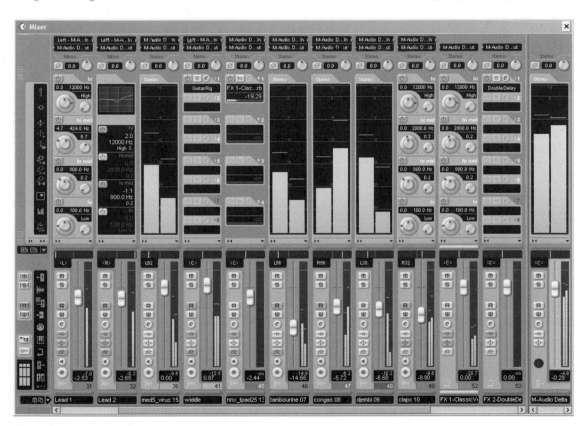

It's also automatable and controllable via MIDI, which means that every function of this mixer has a MIDI address and can be controlled by an external MIDI controller, or you can literally draw controller information onto a track in the arrange window to control volume, panning, anything you like. You want to fade in a track while fading out another, impossible to do with a mouse, so you draw each movement in as automation and the mixer moves by itself. 'Hands free' mixing – it's marvellous.

## Effects

All right then, how about adding all those FX and EQ that make a recording into a gorgeous piece of music?

The advent of 'real-time' processing is what has allowed the PC as a digital recorder to evolve into a virtual studio. Previously to add a delay to an audio track you would have to select the timing and feedback, process that onto the waveform and then, finally, you could hear it back. If it wasn't what you wanted you would have to undo the operation and try again until you got it right, which is a right pain. 'Real-time' means that you can apply an effect directly on a track and alter the parameters while the track is playing and instantly hear the changes, like you would with a hardware effects box. So altering the delay time is simply a matter of moving a knob or slider and you get an immediate response - no more guessing. In the Cubase example the FX and EQ are accessible directly from the mixer and use graphics to give access to controls that go far beyond their real life counterpart (Figure 4.6).

**Figure 4.6**

A bunch of effects including a couple of filters, a convolution reverb, a voice modeller, guitar amp modelling and multiband dynamics.

The effects are overlaid on the audio rather than actually transforming the audio file to create the effect. This means that the effect can be added or removed without destructively editing the actual audio file.

So, does it feel like a studio yet? You've got a mixing desk, you've got fully parametric EQ, you've got a rack of useful effects, all on your PC. That's pretty amazing really.

## Audio track editing

Recording stuff, adding effects and mixing it down is all very well but it's hardly taking advantage of what the hard disk has to offer over tape in the way of editing.

All hard disk recording packages offer some audio editing facilities. For more intense, full-on editing you need to get a dedicated piece of software as described in the next chapter. These can often be used within an audio sequencer, but for now we'll look at the basic functions found in most programs.

Audio editing is applying destructive edits directly onto the waveform (some packages have multiple 'undo' functions which means you can restore the waveform to its original state even after you've edited it to destruction, this can be called non-destructive editing). This enables you to fine-tune the recorded audio. It may be the removal of accidental noises or background noise, cutting off unwanted bits, applying fades, copying and pasting more precisely than in the arrange window, or it may be applying odd effects. Experimentation is the key here.

The usual functions found in this editor are:

- Normalisation – averages out the level across the piece of audio
- Fade in/out
- Reverse
- Change gain – boosting or reducing the overall level
- Silence/mute – reducing a selected part of audio down to silence
- Trim – removing audio around a selection
- Pitch shift/Time stretch – see overleaf

These functions may not make complete sense to you now, but will become more important as you become experienced in hard disk recording. Most are obvious though, like fade in/out (Figure 4.7).

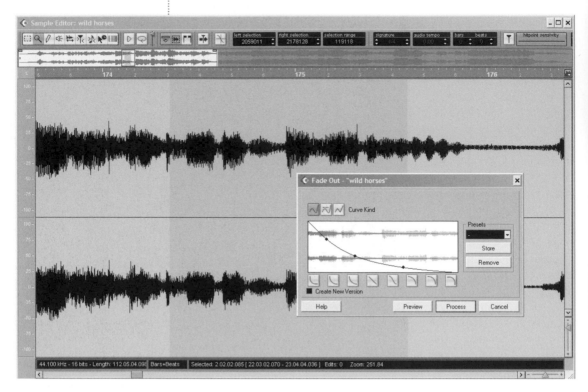

Figure 4.7
Applying a fade out to an audio track in
Cubase.

## Pitch shift and time stretching

Everybody wants to do this and it is a very clever thing that is only possible
within the digital domain. Normally to increase the pitch of something you
speed it up – like spinning a vinyl record too fast. Similarly if you slow something down its pitch will drop. Pitch and time are related which can be a problem when you'd really like to deal with them independently. Changing the
pitch of a digital audio track would speed it up and so then it would no longer
fit in time to the other tracks. Or if you wanted to slow the whole song down
how would you do that without changing the pitch?

Thankfully, the clever programming people came up with some algorithms
(or sets of instructions) which allow pitch and time to be treated separately –
up to a point.

### So, what's this pitch/time stuff about?

You've recorded a vocal track and you'd like to add harmonies. Great, rather
than try to sing them you could make a copy of the track and pitch shift it up
a fifth to create instant harmonies. Pitch shifting technology allows us to keep
the timing the same.

Alternatively you've got two drum loops you want to use but they are
recorded at different bpm (beats per minute). You can stretch one to fit the
other without lowering the pitch.

This all sounds very easy but it's a hard thing to do convincingly. Go 20%
either way and the audio may begin to lose its integrity because the computer is doing a lot of guess work at filling in holes or applying harmonic cor-

rection to prevent the 'pinky and perky' effect.

The simplest use of these tools is for correcting timing and adjusting flat notes. Creating harmonies can be very convincing as long as you don't go too far from the original, and time stretching is most effective on drum loops where pitch is less important. This technology is advancing all the time and just keeps getting better.

Sonar Producer 5 now includes a software version of the Variphrase technology from Roland which allows you to adjust the pitch, formants and timing of vocals completely independently of each other – this is not just 'tweaking', you can re-write whole performances!

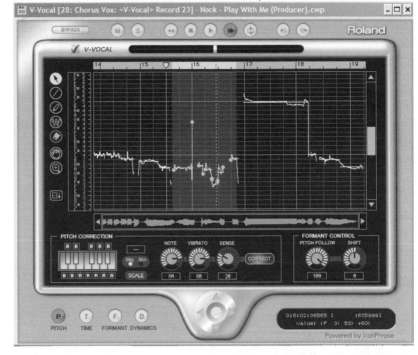

**Figure 4.8**
Roland's V-Vocal Variphrase plug-in in Sonar.

## Summary

Hard disk recording is a fabulous thing. It gives you a live recording studio right in your own home with so much power and potential as to boggle the mind.

The ability to record and mix music is all very well, but to do it well is a skill. Sound engineers train for years before they are good enough to produce really professional sounding albums. They work their way up from making the tea in a studio, spending time learning the recording process, the gear, the way other people work. You can't do it overnight, it takes time and patience, so don't expect your music to suddenly sound of releasable quality. That's why studios cost money to hire, it's not just the equipment, it's the geezer who knows how to work it.

Have a go, see what happens, there's no reason why you can't produce something which sounds half decent and it is completely possible to conceive, record, arrange and master professional sounding music on your home computer. At any rate it'll certainly sound a whole lot better than the recordings you made on that old tape machine.

# Sample/wave editing

This is hard disk recording again in as much as the program allows you to record to hard disk, but it is more often used to edit audio that has already been recorded, to a greater depth than an audio sequencer.

## So, what are the advantages or differences?

This is mainly to do with speed, accuracy and quality. Wave editing packages are designed to deal with very large audio files and many different formats, they are offering, in effect, a mastering and editing suite. It's a place (or in this case a program) where you can apply the finishing touches to a piece of audio, or completely re-edit it, before burning it onto a CD or DVD or compressing it for the internet.

Non-musical applications would be in the form of voice editing, sound effects or Foley editing, soundtrack editing for film, sound analysis and restoration and so on.

You may have recorded a lecture on cassette, DAT or CD. You could dump it into your PC and edit out the coughs or the irrelevant bits, remove background noise and equal out the level.

You may have a bunch of sound effect samples you need to add to a piece of video. You could paste these effects along a time line to match up exactly to the frames of the video.

On a musical level it tools like spectrum and frequency analysis allow you to see how flat your music is across the frequency ranges and where it would really benefit from some EQ. You can use multiband compressors to get your music to the right level for mastering to CD. Finally you have all the tools required to create a master Red Book compliant audio CD that can be used for duplication. CD's contain an eight channel data subcode along with the audio, often called 'P & Q' information (although it goes from P to W) as these are the two most commonly used and important channels. 'P' gives track start time information, or in a continuous piece of music it can be used to mark movements or wherever you would like the CD player to jump to when the skip button is pressed. 'Q' holds the International Standard Recording Code (ISRC) that contains information about the country of origin, the year of publication, owner of the rights, as well as a serial number, and some additional tags like data track mute, and copy protection. Although Windows itself can create audio CDs through Media Player it's not going to let you get that deeply into it. One more cool thing is 'CD Text' which is an extension of the Red Book standard that allows for album and artist name to scroll along the front of a CD player. Creating a CD of your own music and seeing your name appear when you put it in a player is such a pleasing sensation.

**Figure 5.1**
Sony's Sound Forge – a wave editor with an impressive range of features including trimming and cropping, mono/stereo conversion, loop creation tools, EQ, fade envelopes and more.

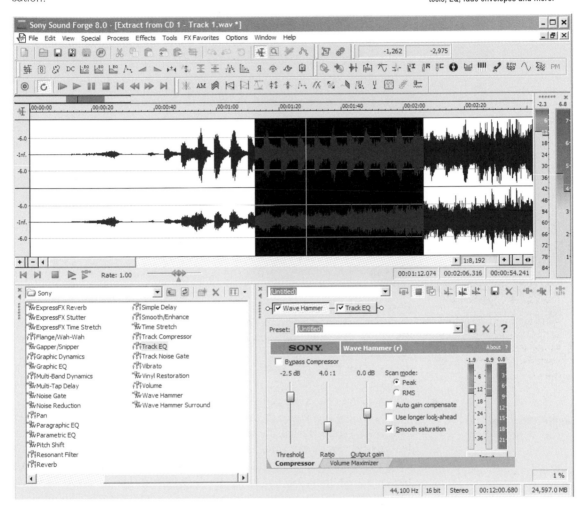

The frequency analysis of one of my recorded songs is shown in Figure 5.2. There is some low frequency rumble around the 20Hz mark. I didn't record any sounds that low so it's probably noise or interference. I may not be able to hear it during the song, but someone else might, and the analysis has enabled me to identify it and remove it with a high pass filter – this is what we like about wave editing programs.

Being able to view an audio file in detail is also invaluable. It's funny how the visual representation of the audio has become almost as important to editing as listening to the actual sound.

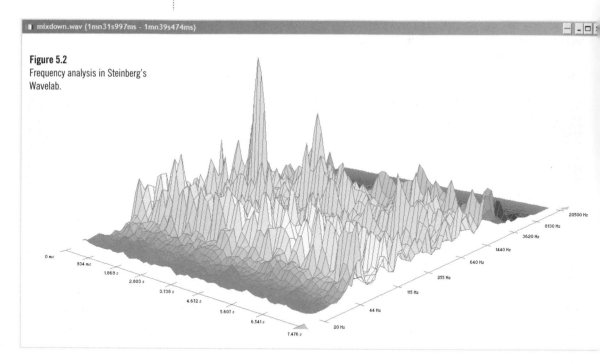

mixdown.wav (1mn31s997ms - 1mn39s474ms)

**Figure 5.2**
Frequency analysis in Steinberg's Wavelab.

## Loops

Audio editors are also useful for creating samples and loops for use in other programs. You have an audio file of a whole piece of music. Within that music there are a number of elements you really like, and you'd like to use them in your own music.

There's this really head crunching snare drum sound that would sound fantastic in a song you're working on, so you can load up the file into the audio editor and search around until you can find a bit where the snare drum is on its own. You highlight it and drag it out so it becomes its own file. Sorted! Now you can paste that snare into your audio sequencer.

Why not take the whole drum section as a loop. If you can find a section of the music where the drums are playing by themselves, highlight it, drag it out, trim it a bit to make sure it works as a loop and bingo, you have a fabulous loop on which to base the rest of your music. It's even possible to detect the main hit points in a loop and automatically determine the bpm. There are many bits of software out there that allow you to create music using simply loops. You can steal these loops off existing music, or, more commonly, get hold of the huge library of ready made loops that exist on purchasable CDs.

It's arguable whether making music from someone else's loops has any creative validity, but it's up to you how you put these sounds together, how you make them work and how creative you can be with them.

Consider scratch DJs making beats and hits using other people's vinyl, this has become a whole art form it itself and has many parallels with loop based work. One artist renowned for his loop based songwriting is Norman Cook from Fat Boy Slim, who is phenomenally successful. It's not the loops that sell the records, it's the creative way he's matched sounds, rhythms and feelings together to produce catchy, commercial tunes.

Always be aware of copyright when using samples or loops from released material in your own work. It's good form to acknowledge where samples originated, but stealing the main riff off a record and using it in your own work can be illegal unless you clear it with the originator first. But hey, we're just having fun right?

**Figure 5.3**
Ableton Live is a composition and performance program built on loops.

## Playlist editing

Programs like Sound Forge have 'Playlist' editing which is a great remixing, or perhaps re-arranging, tool. What it allows you to do is add markers to an audio file and then instruct the program to play back from any of the markers in any order. So you could play back a song, add markers at the first chorus, then the verse, then a couple during the middle 8 etc. Bring up the playlist and instruct the program to play back the chorus twice, then the verse, then the second part of the middle 8, twice, then the chorus three times and so on, completely changing the song. On playback all this jumping around is completely seamless as the hard drive gives, essentially, instant access to any point on the file – another advantage of hard disk recording. The other good thing about playlist editing is that the audio itself hasn't been altered in any way, it's completely non-destructive, so if you don't like your newly edited song, you can change the markers or leave it to playback as it was.

Many people want to use audio editors to remove certain instruments in a piece of music, or edit them separately, or simply extract all the parts back into a multitrack so that they can remix the music themselves. Unfortunately this is not really possible. Once multiple tracks of audio have been mixed together into a single file it's impossible to separate them – it's like trying to remove the eggs once you've baked the cake. A common application of this is to remove the vocals so that track can be used for karaoke – sorry, it's just not going to happen quite as easily as you think.

> **Tip**
>
> The only real way to remix someone else's music is to get hold of the original multitrack recordings.

## Losing the vocals

There are a couple of bits of software that have a go at removing vocals but all they are really doing is applying a filter around the frequency range of the human voice. This can work but it also removes any instruments that sound in those frequencies.

You can also do clever things with phase. Inverting the phase of one side of a stereo track and then recombining them should result in the cancellation of any sound that is dead centre in the mix – usually the vocals. This can work too, but often the remaining track can sound a little strange.

Karaoke functions on music gear such as CD players, PA systems and the like are increasingly common and they often don't do a bad job of quietening the vocal, but it's all a bit of a fudge really and the computer is not really ly going to help. You are better off either recording the song yourself or buying the pre-recorded Karaoke version of it.

# Plug-ins

T his is a great idea and can completely eliminate the need for outboard
equipment that just makes life far simpler.

You may already be familiar with the idea of 'plug-in' filters for graphic programs or for an internet browser. A plug-in is an additional piece of
software that will only function within another piece of software. It literally
plugs into a program to give further facilities.

Hard disk recording plug-ins are often software simulations of real-life
pieces of studio hardware. Compressors, enhancers, noise reduction, parametric EQ, reverb, chorus, delay, filters and amp modellers are among the
plug-ins available. What they do is give you the quality and controls of a real
compressor etc. in software form. So instead of shelling out a load of money
for a Focusrite Red valve compressor you could get the plug-in version and
pay about a quarter of the price. Does it sound the same as the real thing?
Well, yes it does provided the other factors like the quality of inputs and outputs are on the same level. You can't run a microphone through a Sound
Blaster card and through some effects and expect it to sound the same as
running the mic directly through some professional piece of hardware.
However, provided you've got a high quality soundcard or audio interface
then yes software effects can sound every bit as good as hardware ones.
Software has also allowed us to take effects beyond the constraints of hardware into some really weird and creative sound processing.

Most audio recording programs come with a bunch of half decent effects
built in ready to go, however, there are a number of third party manufacturers who do nothing but create effects so if you want the real top notch quality you might have to do a bit of shopping.

One particular plug-in that has been around a while is Antares Auto-Tune.
It's a fascinating piece of software that automatically shifts the pitch of a track
onto the correct notes of a predefined scale. In reality this means that if you
whack it onto a vocal track, the singer will instantly be singing in tune no matter how bad they are. Pop stars don't like to talk about it, but you will find
it's used on a massive number of chart records.

Until recently plug-ins were written specifically for a single program. The
advent of 'DirectX' within Windows and Steinberg's VST (Virtual Studio
Technology) format has allowed third party developers to write software that
can be used by any audio program that supports DirectX or VST, ending
incompatibility annoyances.

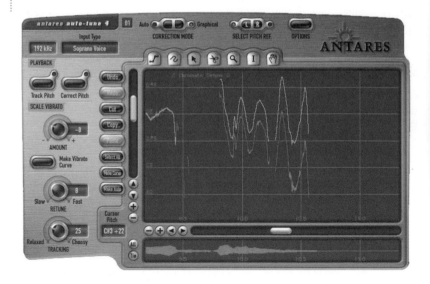

**Figure 6.1**
Antares famous Auto tune for keeping vocalists in line.

**Figure 6.2**
Native Instrument's immensely versatile 'Reaktor' running their 'Space Master' reverb.

Plug-ins can cost a lot more than you think, often matching or exceeding the price of your audio sequencer. You are paying for a great deal of research, development, and the resultant quality, and probably because they think they can get away with it. However, there are loads of independent pro-grammers and enthusiasts out there who like to spend their spare time cre-ating plug-ins and often give them away for free, or maybe ask for a couple of quid. So, whatever effect you're after, from the maddest bit crusher to the lushest reverb you'll find something to do the job – and you'll find links to some of the best ones on my website http://www.pc-music.com

## DSP powered

Before computers were fast enough to run real-time effects the only way to do it was with additional, dedicated cards with on-board DSP (Digital Signal Processors). A card would carry a number of DSP chips that provided a certain amount of processing space for a number of effect plug-ins. These DSP cards were, and still are, the cornerstone of Digidesign's Pro Tools HD system. The great thing about DSP based effects is that they will always be available to you no matter how many tracks of audio or other processing the computer is handling. Once computers began to get faster the increased processing power meant that we could now run effects in real-time without the need for a DSP card, they would run on the 'Host' computer using the CPU to do all the hard maths. The majority of plug-ins are host based and required no additional hardware to run. VST and DirectX are host based formats.

The only restriction on host effects is that they require a certain amount of processing power to run. This same processing power is also trying to share itself between playing back recorded audio, performing any mixing changes, running the graphics engine and the hard disk access, and keeping the general operating system running. Because of this, there's always a trade off. Recording more tracks of audio means that fewer effects can be used, or using lots of effects on one track might mean that you can't use any anywhere else because your computer has reached its processing limit. As you upgrade your computer with more memory etc, then the amount of simultaneous effects available to you will increase.

There are also ways of reducing the processing problem; using a bus effect and routing audio tracks to it, rather than using the same effect on individual inserts, or re-recording a track along with the effect, so that you can then turn the effect off and use it on a different track. You'll soon find the balance between what you want to do and what your computer can handle.

Recently we have seen a desire to return to DSP card based effects again. What with everything, audio, software synths and effects, all being run by the computer, many people want to be sure that they can always have access to a couple of vital effects and not have to worry about balancing and compromise of processing power. This has also been driven by the project studio market who are less likely now to buy into the bottom end of the Pro Tools market, and more likely to go with a host based system like Cubase and a professional audio interface.

Adding a number of effects on a DSP card will make sure that they will always be available regardless of how many audio tracks are running, or how much other processing your computer is occupied with – they are completely processor independent. Their only restriction is the finite power of the DSP chip itself – a single DSP chip might be able to run two effects simultaneously for instance. These two effects will always be available regardless of the track count, but this also means that only two effects are there if you are playing just a single track of audio, whereas there might be room for many more host based effects in this situation.

DSP effects also tend to be proprietary, so that you are stuck with the ones that come with the card, they cannot, unfortunately, run the normal host based effects as well.

**Figure 6.3**
TC Electronic
PowerCore – DSP power
on a PCI card. Also
available as an external
Firewire box.

TC Electronic have produced a DSP card for VST compatible systems called the 'PowerCore'. It comes with effects from their legendary range of hardware processors of a quality only previously available only on expensive Pro Tools systems, but now you can have them running inside Cubase, with no drain on your computer's resources. There's a similar card from Universal Audio. These DSP cards are quite expensive, but then you are getting some very professional tools.

**Figure 6.4**
Noveltech's 'Character' running
on the PowerCore.

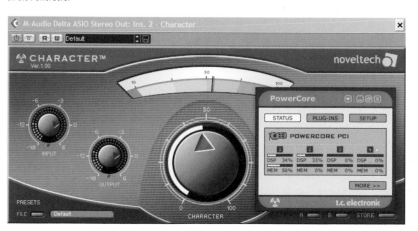

My advice is to use everything. You might find that your soundcard has a DSP chip on-board for running a couple of effects. Fabulous, use them and use your host based effects as well.

If you're a guitarist then you'll find more on guitar effects and amp modelling in the Guitarist's Appendium on page 88.

# Notation and score writing

T hrough MIDI, publishing music has become simple and impressive. No longer do you have to sit at a piano for hours, playing the same phrase over and over while you put marks on a sheet of manuscript. Connect a MIDI keyboard to you PC, play ... and gasp as your whole performance is transcribed instantly.

Even those who can write music off the top of their heads can now put dots on the screen and get an instant playback and/or printout of what they've composed.

It is possible to do full orchestral scoring, 64 staves, and print out a full score as well as individual parts. Text and markings can be added and the layout of the score edited in order to get the printout you're after.

Percussion notation and guitar tabulature can all be included with the relevant note heads and markings, as well as guitar chord symbols and fret diagrams.

Adding lyrics is also a doddle. As you type, the words and syllables automatically arrange themselves under the notes and hyphenate accordingly.

Educational applications are obvious. A student can see instantly how notation relates to the keys being played as the notes appear on the monitor. Complicated pieces of music can be slowed down and played along with, making it easier to learn. Practising with a full orchestra is not an option for everyone, but with notation software the computer could play all the other parts and turn the page (metaphorically speaking) as you play along.

It's the time factor that's most impressive. Anyone who writes musical scores for ensembles containing transposing instruments knows how long it can take to transpose the music for all the instruments. With software it's easy. You can pick an instrument and key from a defined list and the computer will transpose everything for you instantly. Once you've completed the whole score you can extract parts individually and print them out for each musician.

MIDI functionality can often be applied to the same extent as a MIDI sequencer. Controller information can be put onto the stave to correspond to the written dynamics. So when the score says 'p' for 'piano' then there is a corresponding reduction in MIDI velocity. With this kind of control you can get a reasonably accurate performance from the MIDI sounds you are using on playback. The composer no longer has to hire an orchestra in order to get an idea of what his music will sound like

| Tip |
| --- |

M ost manufacturers of notation software offer some form of educational discount so that even impoverished students and teachers can get access to professional scoring software.

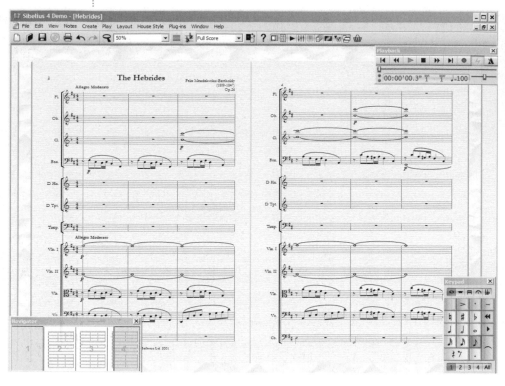

**Figure 7.1**
Sibelius – professional score writing, composition and publishing.

## An orchestra inside?

There's nothing worse than writing a piece of music for a string quartet that sounds fantastic in your head, and then have it crucified by rubbish sounds from the Microsoft GS Wavetable Synth.

If realism is the key then there are a few orchestra focused software instruments that will do an astonishing job of sounding exactly like a real orchestra. East West, previously known for their range of sample CDs have produced a range of software orchestra instruments under the name 'Symphonic Orchestra'. All the individual instruments (strings, woodwind, brass etc.) recorded and sampled in a huge concert hall in order to capture the sound of a real performance. This sort of attention to detail has become with norm with high quality sound sets. This is a long way from a General MIDI 'Strings' patch. The other option is to use a software sampler such as GigaStudio from Tascam where you can load up an orchestral sound set of realistic instruments to play back your music. The sample sizes offered by software samplers mean that the instrument sounds can be sampled multiple times, in multiple ways and end up sounding incredibly realistic and dynamic.

A quick comparison would be that GigaStudio ships with a piano sound created using 1 gigabytes worth of samples. The Microsoft GS Wavetable Synth probably has 128 sounds that are created using about 2 megabyte's worth of samples in total. You can purchase CD/DVD-ROM's containing ready made orchestral instruments with every nuance and playing style available to you. So, you can now have an orchestra sitting inside your computer giving you an instant performance of your work.

**Info**

See page 50 for more information on software samplers.

## But don't you have to be a very accurate player to get decent results?

Well, yes to a degree, the more accurate your playing the less editing you'll have to do afterwards. The more professional programs do have the ability to cope with sloppy playing rather well. Sibelius (a top end notation program shown in Figure 7.1) will sense variations in tempo and adapt accordingly. Other programs use a footswitch to dictate the tempo so you can vary as much as you like.

Figure 7.2
Tascam's GigaStudio for amazingly realistic orchestral sounds

## Scanning

A recent advance in scoring technology is that of scanning. Optical character recognition (OCR) has got to the stage where a piece of manuscript can be scanned into the computer and the individual notes are recognised by the program. So you can now scan in an old piece of music and get the computer to play it back. Or you could transpose the scanned piece of music, print it out, and give it to your trombone player. You could even archive old manuscripts (after making any copyright considerations) and print them out at your leisure.

Notation software does for written music what word processing did for typing. With the technology of printers always increasing, the quality of print out is instantly publishable. It's never been quicker or easier to work on your masterpiece.

# Software instruments – synthesis and sampling

F or as long as computers have had soundcards they've also had some kind of synthesiser built in. Usually a General MIDI compliant set of uniformly awful sounds that are there to playback MIDI files in Windows – useful, but not exactly inspiring. Besides, these were FM based or wavetable sounds with no editing facilities of any kind which sort of defeated the object of 'synthesis'.

## General MIDI (GM)

A standard that defines what instrument sounds are assigned to which MIDI patch or program numbers. So, on a GM MIDI device the first sound will always be 'Piano'. It also specifies that drum kit sounds must appear on MIDI channel 10, and conform to a specific layout across the keyboard. This is useful as it allows a piece of music created on one GM device to be played back on another and come out sounding correct. The original specification allowed for 128 sounds plus 10 drum kits. Roland and Yamaha have gone further to produce their own expanded versions of GM, which are still backwardly compatible with the original spec. Roland's GS standard offers around 250 sounds, and also adds control for reverb and chorus effects. Yamaha's XG standard goes further still, with over 700 sounds, a few more drum kits and lots of controls for all kinds of effects. Most software sequencers allow you to select a GM sound by name, which is a lot more friendly than having to select sounds by bank and program numbers.

In 1997 a small Scandinavian software company called Propellerhead released a little music program that revolutionised the computer music industry overnight. The program was called Rebirth RB-338 and was a beautiful simulation of a pair of Roland TB-303 bass synths and a TR-808 rhythm machine. It looked fantastic and sounded even better. Suddenly you could be the Chemical Brothers without having to invest thousands of pounds in vintage synth equipment. It's amazing how two single oscillator mono synths and simple drum machine could have such an effect. You couldn't even play them from a keyboard, the TB-303 used a step sequencer and the TR-808 used a row of 16 pads that you could turn on or off for each sound as it cycled through. This was precisely why Rebirth was such a success. At that time computer and soundcard technology was not up to the task of generating sound fast enough from software to make using a keyboard viable. Rebirth bypassed this problem completely by making it step-sequenced.

The success of Rebirth spawned two important technologies. Steinberg, creators of Cubase had recently released their Virtual Studio Technology (VST) architecture which brought proper 'live' mixing and real-time effects plug-ins to their recording software. Propellerhead wanted to find a way to use Rebirth alongside, or integrated into the VST engine. What they came up with was 'Rewire'. This was essentially a bridge between the outputs of Rebirth and the VST mixer in Cubase so you could route, mix and effect Rebirth alongside audio tracks. At the same time Steinberg was working on another technology, an extension of their VST engine that allowed them to plug-in software synths like they did with effects. These were called VST Instruments or VSTi's. The success of VSTi's hinged on the seemingly elusive ability to play them, in real time, from a MIDI keyboard. Steinberg's driver technology ASIO (Audio System In/Out) was the key but it wasn't quite fast enough yet. Working hard with a handful of soundcard manufacturers they released ASIO 2.0 and VST 2.0 in 1999 which, for the first time, managed to get latency down to under the 10ms (milliseconds) mark which rendered VSTi's, at last, totally playable. Steinberg also released their 'Developers Kit'

**Figure 8.1**
Propellerhead's Rebirth RB338 – two classic Roland analogue synths and drum machines in virtual form.

**Figure 8.2**
ASIO, VST and Rewire, three entwined technologies.

free of charge so that anyone with the desire and programming skills could create their own VSTi's and VST effects. As a result there are hundreds and hundreds of freeware and shareware plug-ins as well as fully fledged, professionally produced, commercial ones.

## Latency

This is really something quite simple and shouldn't grip people with the kind of fear it appears to. Latency is the amount of time between a call and a response. In computer music terms this is the amount of time it takes for the computer to generate a sound when asked to. In practical terms it's the time between clicking 'Play' and playback starting, or it's the time between hitting a key on a keyboard and hearing the sound from the computer, or it's the time between plucking a string on a guitar and hearing the sound though the computer, with effects. In the bad old days you were talking about latencies of half a second or more which meant trying to play anything 'live' was a joke (try it yourself with the Microsoft GS Wavetable Soft Synth and you'll understand). These days, with the right soundcard, latency is so small that you don't notice it and playing sounds on a computer has become as live as any other instrument.

Latency is a natural function of computers, a built in delay to allow the CPU to process information and get it out in an ordered fashion. The delay is caused by a 'buffer' which is a small piece of memory where information to be processed is stored and sorted. As data (or sound) comes in it fills the buffer while the CPU sorts it out, processes it and sends it in a constant stream to the outputs. The larger the buffer, the larger the delay/latency, the smoother the output. So for 'real-time' processing we want that buffer as small as we can make it, however, this puts added pressure on the CPU as it has to work faster to maintain the same smooth output. If the data moves through the buffer too quickly then the CPU may not have time to sort it out and you end up with a glitch or crackle in the audio. You can see that there's a bit of a balancing act going on.

Generally, when playing instruments, a latency of 10ms or less is regarded as real-time. When mixing 30ms is completely fine so you'll find that you can reduce the stress on the computer when mixing by increasing the soundcards buffer size resulting in stable playback and room for more effects – magic! To benefit from low latencies it's essential that you have a soundcard or audio interface with drivers designed to do it.

If you have a regular soundcard, using Windows multimedia drivers, the normal latency is going to be 750ms, that's 3/4 of a second! It's so important, not just for soft synths but for your whole computer studio, to get a soundcard or audio interface that has fast and well written ASIO drivers – everything will simply work much better. Cubase is not the only program to support ASIO, VSTi's or VST effects. Cakewalk's Sonar also supports the ASIO protocol as well as taking advantage of Microsoft's improved WDM Windows drivers and DirectSound facilities in their DirectX multimedia utility and so is fully compatible with VSTi's as well as DirectX instruments (Dxi). Many shareware programs are also fully compatible. The only major commercial program that isn't compatible is Digidesign's Pro Tools that uses their own format called RTAS (Real-Time Audio Suite).

Now you know what we're talking about let's have a look at a few.

## Software synthesisers

I don't think there's any form of synthesis left now that can't be done on computer. Analogue, wavetable, subtractive, additive, granula, vector, acoustic modelling and more I haven't thought of yet. The driving force behind many software synth innovations has been German company Native Instruments. One of their first releases was a model of the legendary Sequential Circuits Prophet 5. Looks superb and sounds amazing and is exactly like the real thing. The current version called the Pro 53 adds various cool enhancements.

**Figure 8.3**
Native Instrument's Pro 53 – a model of the legendary Sequential Circuits Prophet 5.

With the rest of the industry focused on producing analogue style synths NI then released a model of the Hammond B3 organ they called the B4, and again, it's perfect. From there NI produced synths like the peculiar Absynth and the extraordinary Reaktor that have no basis in anything in the real world as far as I can see. Reaktor lets you build completely new synths from the tiniest building blocks or just use the wealth of synths created by other users. They also managed to produce the synth that Yamaha wouldn't, called the FM7, based of course upon the famous DX7 and it was even capable of loading old DX7 patches.

Many people had been producing simple analogue style farty bass synths in a Minimoog style but it wasn't until French company Arturia pulled their Minimoog V out of the bag that the legendary Dr Moog was happy to put his

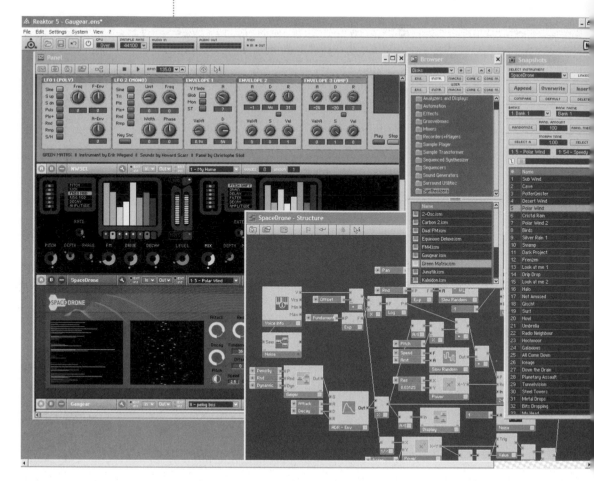

**Figure 8.4**
Native Instruments extraordinary 'Reaktor.

name to it. On the release of their Moog Modular V Dr Moog said 'Arturia's Moog Modular V is a high quality computer emulation of the analog modular synthesizer that Moog Music® originally introduced... I am delighted that Arturia's Moog Modular V is adding a new dimension to an instrument tradition that has a special meaning to so many musicians.' Arturia have since moved on to the Yamaha CS-80 and Arp2600. It's interesting to note how important the visual look and feel has become. I've heard many great software synths that have failed because the interface didn't look that great.

## Workhorse sound modules

Hardware manufacturers like Roland, Korg and Yamaha have resisted releasing software versions of their synths, so other companies have done it for them. Korg at least is getting with the program a bit with its superb Legacy Collection, software versions of the MS-20, Polysix and Wavestation, and the Digital Collection that adds the famous M1. The Trinity and Triton, though, remain for the moment hardware only. If you are after a Sound Canvas type module, like a Roland JV1080 or Korg Trinity then check out Sampletank and Sonik Synth from IK Multimedia and Hypersonic from Steinberg. These are

**Figure 8.5**
Arturia's Moog Modular V — a work of art.

Figure 8.6
IK Multimedia's Sampletank 2, a
workhorse sound module with more
sounds than you could ever need.

huge synths concentrating on the kind of mass market sounds made popular
by the hardware.

## Software samplers

If there's one area where the hardware market has been completely deci-
mated by software then it's sampling. The sampler has been a vital part of
any studio for some twenty years, allowing the use of real instrument sounds,
loops, hits and snatched performances in music production. An entire industry emerged creating CD's of samples for your sampler, everything from sax-
ophones to dripping taps, break beats to footsteps on shingle. In the space
of a couple of years the two main hardware sampler players Emu and Akai
would all but disappear. The main culprit was GigaStudio from Nemesys
Music, now part of Tascam. Its killer technology was that it could use the
computer's hard disk to store and stream samples. The first version allowed
for sample sizes up to 4GB's (gigabytes) in size. At that time hardware samplers commonly used 32MB's of RAM for samples so the difference was staggering. Normally, if you wanted to create a sample of a real instrument you
would record that instrument playing a couple of notes and put that into the
sampler. The sampler would then speed up or slow down the sample to cover
the notes in between. You may also make recordings at different strengths
(or velocity levels) as the sound changes depending on how hard you play,
but with only a few megabytes of space there were limits. With GigaStudio
came the GigaPiano which was an instrument made up of 1GB's worth of
samples. Each note on the piano was individually sampled and at multiple

velocity levels giving an amazing amount of realism. As GigaStudio developed and other similar software samplers arrived, hardware samplers simply couldn't compete. I've installed GigaStudio systems into studios that have replaced entire racks of hardware samplers. To add insult to injury GigaStudio is completely compatible with hardware sampler formats so after a day of copying library across to the computer it is all instantly accessible off hard disk, no more searching around for that sample you had somewhere on a badly labelled floppy disk.

**Figure 8.7**
Native Instruments Kontakt sampler.

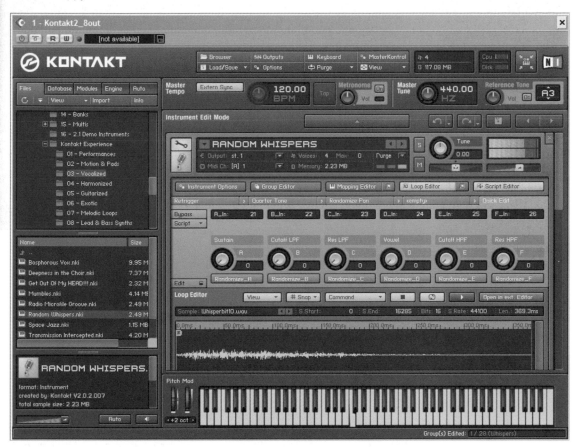

The main software sampler players other than GigaStudio are Kontakt from Native Instruments and Halion from Steinberg. Emu have recently rejoined the show as part of Creative Labs and have produced a range of professional music soundcards that include the EmulatorX software sampler that's a direct descendant from their hardware samplers. Akai manage to hold on in the hardware market thanks to the live performance, hip hop and DJ markets. Their MPC range of samplers feature pads and built in sequencers for an altogether different beat making experience. All the software samplers come with DVDs packed with sample libraries, some of them containing the most amazingly sampled orchestral sounds. It is now possible to produce a completely convincing orchestral performance with sample libraries like the massive Vienna Symphonic Library and sample CD producer

EastWest's Symphonic Orchestra. Fantastic for the composer, being able to hear what his music will sound like without hiring an orchestra, but bad for orchestras and orchestral musicians? Maybe, maybe not. Talking to the ever level headed David Arnold, composer for many films including all the recent Bond movies, he finds that the quality of these libraries enables him to show the producers how good a real orchestra would sound before they invest in the process of doing it for real. This has resulted in more work for real musicians rather than less.

## Romplers

That's not a real term but it's the best way to describe this wing of software instruments. These mainly come from the companies that used to produce sample CD's. Rather than just selling the sounds for importing into your software sampler they've bolted them into their own software instrument interface so you can instantly play and use all the sounds and samples in your recording software. There's no editing, sampling or synthesis going on, just the sounds with perhaps a filter or envelope effect, so they are essentially 'Read Only' samplers or 'Romplers'. This has resulted in a torrent of released from EastWest, Best Service, Zero-G and many more. Some are simply back catalogue re-releases whereas others are beefed up into new and useful collections of samples, loops and instruments.

## Reason

After living the high life on the success of Rebirth, the Propellerhead team locked themselves in a cupboard for a couple of years and emerged bleary eyed with another awesome piece of software. 'Reason' takes their love of analogue gear and forges it with sampling, mixing, effects and sequencing to create a whole dance music studio in the one program. You have a subtractive synth, a Graintable synth, a sampling drum machine, two digital samplers, dozens of effects and the 'Dr:Rex' which is a loop chopping machine similar to their other successful product 'Recycle'. You can run as many of each instrument as you like, you can create patterns like in Rebirth using the 'Matrix' sequencer or use pure MIDI sequencing, you have MIDI control over every parameter and pump it all into a big virtual mixer with EQ and effects. It's a fabulous sound source that gets you bouncing around to cool tunes in a matter of minutes. It looks like a rack of analogue synths, but this is only half the story. Turn the rack around and you'll find a mess of virtual cables patching everything together in an old fashioned 'CV/Gate' kind of way. You can re-patch anything into anything else, so you could use a drum pattern to trigger the sampler, or the LFO on a synth to vary the filter on the sampler, keeps you fascinated for hours.

## Acoustic modelling

It seems as if each new software synth pushes back some more boundaries, and it's become such a popular format that there are hundreds of freeware and shareware VSTi's out there that it all becomes a bit mind boggling. Standing out from the crowd is getting to be a challenge in itself. Choosing a different form of synthesis is one way to get noticed and 'acoustic modelling' always raises a few eyebrows.

Yamaha had a go at this with their VL technology found in a couple of their hardware synths. The idea is to build a computer model of how acoustic instruments generate sound. So, you'd model a vibrating string, or a hammer, and then model the resonator – like the guitar body or tube of a flute. This can create some wonderfully expressive and realistic sounds. An example would be that the computer holds a model of all the acoustical properties of a wind instrument, how the air vibrates, the affect of the instruments material. Apply to this a similar model of a bowed string instrument and the result would be an accurate representation of a bowed flute, if such a thing was possible. The possibilities of sound creation are limitless. Applied Acoustics have created 'Tassman', which is the best example of this kind of synthesis, but in a very analogue and funky way. You take hammers and beams, strings and resonators and treat them like you would oscillators. You stick in a load of other models of filters and LFO's and can end up creating some fascinating sounds, from fat synth basses to spooky wind sounds and plucked glass.

**Figure 8.8**
Part of the front and back of the rack of synths and devices available in Propellerhead's Reason.

## Control

In the late 1980's when digital synths became smooth, black slabs, with two buttons and a horribly complicated, page based, editing system on a small screen, people went searching for the old analogue synths in pure frustration. People wanted tactile interaction, knobs and sliders to move which responded immediately. Editing which was obvious and easy. Modern synths are covered with such knobs in response to these demands. So, taking all that hardware we love fiddling with and dumping it onto a computer controlled by a single mouse, seems a little foolish to me. One of the biggest complaints against ReBirth is that you can only move a single control at a time. In response, new MIDI controllers, bits of hardware with knobs on that send out MIDI controller information, have been designed to work with computer based synths, so you can now fiddle with real knobs in ReBirth. Most MIDI controller keyboards you can get these days come bristling with knobs and sliders and often have preset templates for some of the more popular synths like Reason. This is a great development, although you are back to having a load of external gear again!

**Figure 8.9**
Korg's Kontrol 49 keyboard controller with knobs, faders and pads for complete MIDI control over synths and drum machines.

Software instruments are so much fun and give you fabulous sounds that you only dreamed of before. They offer so many exciting features and quality for a lot less money that the hardware counterpart. They can also offer functions and sonic treats that were never possible before.

To top it all off Propellerhead discontinued Rebirth and have released it into the world as a free download from http://www.rebirthmuseum.com – how cool is that?

# Internet music

If ever there was a perpetually evolving technology then the internet is it. I am constantly surprised by new developments and it becomes increasingly hard to keep track. The beauty (although this beauty is fast being eroded by commercialism) is that the internet is (was) driven largely by enthusiasts, people with a passion for what they doing, a desire to be heard. The World Wide Web (WWW) is a global publishing house allowing the user to share their thoughts, ideas and their music with the world. No management required, no agents, no permission, no signed piece of paper. By putting your music on the web you become a published artist. Sounds good doesn't it?

I'm not about to show you how to create html documents for publishing music, that information is freely available over the internet. What I will do is show you some of the tools being used and what they could mean for your music, that way if you wanted to have a go you would at least know what to look for and what is currently possible. Although, the use of 'currently' in this context refers to what's happening at the time of writing, by the time you actually read this then things may be rather different. It just means that the picture will hopefully be even rosier than the one I'm currently painting.

## MIDI files

The first format of music to be shared over the internet was the MIDI file. A song created with a MIDI sequencer that can be played back through a MIDI device. MIDI files are very small, typically under 100kB and so are quick to download. Bulletin boards are filled with MIDI files of famous songs and original works. It's staggering how much work can go into those MIDI files of famous songs. The creator must spend hours working on the arrangement until every track is spot on the original. Others, it must be said, are appalling.

With General MIDI available on every computer with the Microsoft GS Wavetable Synth, the MIDI file you downloaded will sound pretty much as the writer intended. So, you write your MIDI music, post the file on the internet, and anyone with access can download and listen to your music through the Microsoft synth on their own system. Groovy. There is a niggling problem with this though, partly to do with the Microsoft synthesiser, and partly do to with ignorance. If you're a musician and you've got a couple of decent MIDI devices or software instruments then your music will probably sound really good running through your quality synthesiser or whatever. When an adoring fan downloads the file they will hear it played back through the Microsoft synth and so it will probably sound rubbish. So, although the music arrangement will sound as intended, the actually quality of the sounds will vary depending on the MIDI device being used for playback. Unfortunately many people are not aware of this and the listener may assume that what they are hearing is a real recording of your music, rather than a MIDI file playing through their own system. Subsequently they may tell you that your music is terrible for all the wrong reasons.

So what you really want is to get an actual recording of your music playing off the internet – now we're talking about MP3.

## So what is an 'MP3'?

**Figure 9.1**
Remember this?

It's amazing how such a small thing can cause such a ruckus and strike fear into the heart of the mega music corporations. I'm reminded of the 'Home Taping Is Killing Music' campaign that was slapped around back in the early 1980's – it didn't and I don't believe it will. The music industry is certainly changing and there will be casualties along the way but once the dust settles the corporations will still be in charge but hopefully with a greater respect for the consumer.

MP3's are a type of audio file, very similar to wave files, except they have a much smaller file size due to the fact that they have been very cleverly compressed. This has nothing to do with dynamics compression used on audio in mixing and recording, this is about data compression, like using a 'zip' file. The compression is clever because it reduces the file size without reducing the quality of the audio (arguably, oh and people do like to argue). The file you end up with has the extension '.mp3' the same as a wave file has the extension '.wav'. That's where the name comes from. Windows often hides these extensions in case they scare somebody and instead gives the file a friendly icon to represent the file type.

MP3 is the file extension for 'MPEG audio layer 3', MPEG being the 'Moving Pictures Expert Group' who are a bunch of people who go around trying to compress things, like video and audio, in order to make them more manageable for computers and the internet. Audio files are big, well at least in terms of the internet. CD Quality audio, 16bit 44.1kHz in stereo uses up 10MB per minute, so a three minute song would be 30MB. A whole album would be, funnily enough, a whole CD's worth which is about 640MB. It follows that to make the audio files smaller you could use a lower resolution like 8bit or 22kHz but this would drastically reduce the quality of the sound.

But why would you want to reduce the size of your audio files? Well, the internet is a global publishing house. Started off with text, your text for the world to read, then images, pictures of stuff and then it became sophisticated enough to hold sound, video and other media. So you can publish your music on the net for people around the world to download and listen to. Now, your 3 minute, 30MB, potential hit, song is huge in internet terms. If you were using a regular 56k modem (I know you've all got Broadband these days but bear with me) it could download probably half a MB per minute (with the wind behind you), so it could take easily an hour to download a single 3 minute song of CD quality. That would have to be one very devoted fan to wait that long. To make publishing audio on the internet a reality we had to find a way of reducing the file size, but without reducing the quality.

In 1995 the Fraunhofer Institute, in Germany, concentrated their efforts on purely audio encoding (all other MPEG standards have involved video) and came up with MP3, 'CD quality' at a $12^{th}$ of the size of the original. So rather than an hour it might take just 6 minutes. With a Broadband connection it might take half a minute, or even better it would just playback, in real-time, straight off the web page, so suddenly people have instant access to your music.

So how do they do that then? The MP3 format uses perceptual audio coding and psychoacoustic compression to remove all superfluous information. What this means is that it removes all the stuff in the file that you don't really hear anyway, high and low frequencies that your ears can't detect and other clever bits of psychoacoustic skulduggery. The result is astounding and, to the untrained ear, sounds the same as the original. It's more accurately referred to as 'near CD quality'. This is of course where all the fuss about copyright and the death of the music industry comes in. People could take commercial CD's and convert them to MP3, this is perfectly legal for you own use, but then they could email them to their friends who would, near as damn it, have a perfectly good sounding copy. Not only that but the use of file sharing programs, brought into being by the likes of 'Napster', allowed complete strangers to share their entire CD collections online for anyone to download. So, theoretically one person could buy the CD and within a few minutes everyone in the world could have a copy. Outrageous and, of course, completely illegal.

**Figure 9.2**
Napster's logo.

I'll put my hand up and admit to file sharing MP3s via Napster back in the late 1990s. It wasn't so much about getting music for free as to hearing tunes you hadn't heard for ages, or always fancied listening to but would never buy the CD. In actual fact I found myself buying more CD's after rediscovering a load of music through downloads. It was also how I contracted my first computer virus that wiped my entire hard drive clean in front of my very eyes – twice. Napster was forced to shut down in 2001 as a result of court action by the Record Industry Association of America (RIAA) and has since re-emerged as a perfectly legal music subscription service.

There's a feeling on the internet that all music should be free. There should be an end to record companies taking our money, dictating what we should listen to and restricting access to wider forms of music. Instead you have a huge library of music that would stream off the internet directly to your computer, or even to your hi-fi. That's fine but who's going to be making all this music? If it ends up being home studio enthusiasts like ourselves then, let's face it, the quality will fall through the floor. Also there will be so much available that we would drown under the weight of rubbish music, desperately searching for a decent track. Record companies, love them or loathe them, provide a filtering system for getting rid of the rubbish (obviously subjective) and also provide investment in artists so they can give up their day job and spend their time making music and improving on their craft. There is already a wealth of legally free music out there. A number of websites have sprung up promoting new music and new artists providing a focal point or a launch pad for anyone wanting to get their music heard.

I was always of the opinion that MP3 was a temporary technology, a workaround way of making music downloadable at a reasonable quality but as the internet got faster then people would want the full fat, high quality, wave files. But as the poor sales of DVD-Audio and SACD have shown few people are that interested in pristine audio quality and they would rather squeeze 200 MP3's onto a CD than 5 minutes of DVD quality surround sound.

## iPods, iTunes and Napster 2

With all the confusion, allegations, threats and fear surrounding the MP3 format it took a mighty company with a steady hand to cut through the rubbish and provide a money making opportunity – cue Apple. Everything about the iPod is a work of genius, the marketing, the cool factor, the design and the product itself. The iPod made digital music cool and iTunes made selling it easy. If you're not familiar (and you'll be the only one who isn't) then the iPod is like the old Sony Walkman but instead of cassette you have a little hard disk onto which you can fit about 20,000 MP3 size songs. The beauty is that you can rip your entire CD collection onto your iPod, select 'shuffle' and listen for the rest of your life. For many people, bored with radio, out of touch with the hit parade, it brought music back into their lives. iTunes is an accompaniment to the iPod and is like one big music shop where rather than selling CD's they sell individual tracks for download, for like 79p each, straight onto your iPod. They have millions of tracks to choose from with more being added all the time. Each track has a 30 second preview so you can try before you buy – genius, although not as cheap as everyone would like.

Figure 9.3 The Apple iPod family of MP3 and media players.

I was suspicious of the new Napster that arrived in the UK in 2004. I had a poke around and as with iTunes I bought a few individual tracks. It was quite cool creating your own compilation CD's and then buying them, but it was the idea of subscription that gave me a sinking feeling. You would pay a tenner, per month, and then you could download and listen to anything you liked – great, however, if you stop your subscription the music collection you've been building up would cease to be. My wife, tired of my moaning about it, goes and buys me a subscription to Napster for Christmas which also allows me to transfer the downloads to my Creative Labs MP3 player. Well, it's bloody marvellous. I can lose myself for days searching for interesting things to listen to, leaping from one album via a recommendation to something completely different, picking up those old tracks I always meant to buy along the way. Slap a dozen or so albums on the MP3 player and we're set for any journey. One criticism often levelled at these sorts of services is that with 1.6 million tunes to choose from aren't you going to have to trudge through an awful lot of rubbish before you find something worth listening to? This could be true but Napster have provided built in quality filters in the guise of recommended playlists, some from themselves but others from featured artists, or newspapers or magazines. They have charts of every kind and every genre so you're not faced with just a very very long list of tracks. Interestingly Napster uses the Microsoft 'wma' compression format which includes the technology it needs to make subscription work. Sound quality is arguably better and Microsoft can constantly improve it within the same format whereas MP3 is stuck somewhat by its own standards but it's far more compatible and cross platform whereas wma is Windows only.

**Figure 9.4**
Napster's online subscription service.

## Your music as MP3

For a couple of years the dream that the internet would produce a number of new, independent, successful artists flew around. You don't need record companies, you simply upload your tunes and pretty soon, word gets around and you're scooping up the royalties. Problem is that the chances of anyone stumbling across your music are ludicrously minute, and it's even more unlikely that anyone would actually want to pay for it if they did find it. There were websites where you could upload your music, like mp3.com, giving you more chance of being heard but copyright allegations and the difficulty in making any money from it ultimately sealed the fate for internet based bedroom to stadium stardom dreamers. On the other hand if people have a reason to buy your music then the internet is the perfect outlet. Your website could be an extension of your usual marketing. Along with your gigs, your CD's on sale, t-shirts, everything should be available online so that anyone who finds themselves in possession of a flyer can see what you're about, when you next play and of course hear your music. Personally I like the idea that's emerged of promoting your music with a couple of freebie downloads and then sell a real CD off the back of them. Using wonderful online credit card services like PayPal, and even using an eBay shop, you can take orders and sell without all the hassle of setting up companies and talking to VISA. In fact I bought a CD called Bimbling by Martha Tilston in exactly that way just last week. You see I still like physical product. I like the artwork, the album cover, the whole physical experience, and the fact that the music is mine to do with as I will.

## Creating your own MP3

Most recording software comes with MP3 encoding built in. When you come to mixing down you can opt to export the mix as a MP3 file. There are various levels of compression and sound quality available in MP3 encoding which affect the file size. 128kbps (kilo bytes per second) is the accepted 'near CD quality' standard that's good enough for most people. Personally I can sometimes hear the squashing of high frequencies, especially on cymbals, and so using 256kbps tends to sort that out, although it doubles the file size. The key is to get over your own critical listening and go with what the people want.

## Podcasting

Just when you think you've got all corners covered along comes a new way of getting your stuff out there. This is not the chance meeting of a mouse across a webpage, this is deliberate, searched for, on-demand, subscription to your music. – this is podcasting.

Podcasting enables anyone to create their own radio show that can be searchable on iTunes (and elsewhere) subscribed to and downloaded. The key thing is this – you upload your next podcast (which is essentially an MP3 file), as soon as a subscriber opens iTunes the new podcast will automatically be downloaded to their desktop or dumped to their iPod. For the listener this means that you subscribe to something you like and you will automatically receive the next edition without having to look for it or actively download it. For us it means that we don't have to keep getting people back to our website, we just release the next one and our subscribers are automatically updated – how cool is that? It's not a broadcast, it's not time sensitive, people can discover your podcast at any time and download earlier ones or simply subscribe from the latest one onwards. Add to that the support for images, descriptions, web links, keywords and categories all tied up in the RSS file and you can start to see how it moves beyond any other form of internet distribution.

A number of different factors and internet technologies came together and found their ultimate outward expression in podcasting. It was almost like this had been what everyone was building towards. Blogging had shown that everyone was a writer, a journalist, everyone had a voice and desire to get it out there. iPods had brought MP3 to the masses and introduced whole generations of people to digital music held on computer rather than CD. RSS had made the idea of subscribed 'pushed' content possible and easy.

The radio analogy has made people realise an MP3 doesn't have to be music – it can be speech, or in fact any audio at all. 'Audioblog' podcasts abound, although it's harder to sound intelligent when speaking than it is when writing, a problem being overcome by feed2podcast.com who provide a Stephen Hawking style computerised reading of your blog. Podcasts have become the ideal vehicle for lectures, tutorials, sermons and preaching – every Sunday you can push a podcast of your service to all the members of your congregation who couldn't attend, or who would like to study it further. Same goes for students, training and teaching in all sorts and all forms.

Coming back to your music, why would you have an MP3 available to download off your website when instead you could have a podcast, listed on iTunes, keyword, genre and category searchable, embedded with images and links, and when you release a new track everyone who listened to your first one will automatically receive the new one. Why not hook up with a few other artists, combine a number of tunes into a bit of a radio show and create a weekly or monthly podcast. As a listener, if someone sent you an hour of consistently good music (as yours undoubtedly is) every week, which required no action on your part, then you would probably tell your friends about it.

**Info**

RSS or 'Really Simple Syndication' crops up all over the internet these days and although it's hard to pin on an exact definition it allows you publish information that can be updated and 'pushed' to anyone who subscribes – it's often called a 'web feed' and is commonly used by news websites.

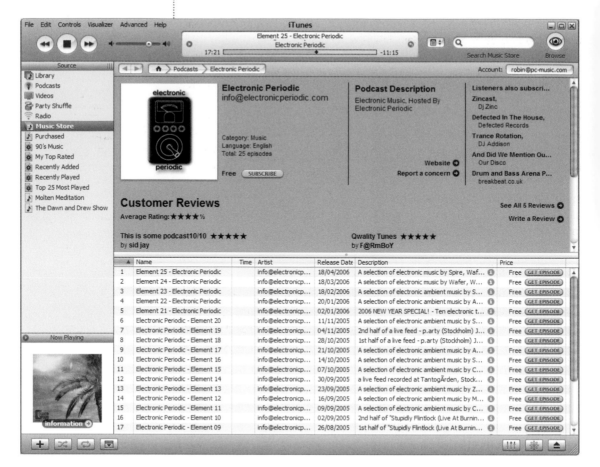

**Figure 9.5**
Podcasts in Apple's iTunes.

## MP3 alternatives

### RealAudio

Apart from MP3, the other major player is a company called Real Networks. Their RealAudio format has been around a while and has been responsible for improving the possibilities of music distribution on the internet. It uses a similar compression format to MP3 in that it can reduce the size of an audio file to one 15th of its original size with little loss in quality. Where RealAudio differs is in the ability to stream directly off the internet and play back in real time. Using the Real Player you can click on a music file and it begins to download. After a few seconds the file begins to play back while the rest is still downloading. Cool, no more hanging around waiting for a download. The latest versions of the Real Player can also show embedded video and graphics at the same time.

### *Quicktime*

The other compression format of note is Apple's Quicktime format. Widely used by the film industry as a means of showing trailers to films online. Apple have come up with (or borrowed) an incredible compression format called the 'Qdesign codec'. You are probably familiar with Quicktime movies and the like, well, the current version has the capability of streaming near CD quality audio off a web page on a standard 56kps modem connection. The quality is rather good. There's something not quite right though. It does sound good, but you can tell that something has happened to it, like it's been recorded in a dustbin or something. This is particularly noticeable with real instruments, acoustic guitar, cymbals, that sort of thing. I have a composer/musician friend who has used Quicktime to squash a 70MB audio file, of mainly electronic music, down to almost 1MB and it sounds great. Again, with broadband connections the quality has increased greatly as the compression doesn't need to be so severe.

The technology for internet music distribution, in terms of connection speed and the quality of software compression, is improving all the time. We already have internet radio, internet TV, and video 'on demand' all at 'acceptable' quality. It's an exciting place to be.

## Sticking with MP3

The cheapest and easiest way to publish your music on the internet in my opinion is still MP3. All the software is free, the quality is great and it's all created by enthusiasts. New formats are regularly being touted around promising to bring even better quality sound with greater compression but MP3 just seems to stick.

# Intermission

Phew! That's a load of information to take on board all at once. Crack open a beer, light a cigarette and take a moment to consider everything so far.

Do you know what you want to do yet?

I hope, at least, that you now have some rudimentary understanding of what a PC can do for music. It all comes down to what you want to get out of this. Experiment and have fun, that's what this is all about. I could give you every example in the book, lead you step by step through the creative process, but it would be my creative process, yours may be vastly different. All the programs on offer give you the tools to create, it is up to you how you use them.

The products will all change and evolve over time as the stampede of technology cuts a swathe towards the future. Things that seem out of reach or impossible now will soon become simple. It's an exciting industry to be involved with, and the tools on offer can add a whole new perspective to the creative process, or just simply let you have fun.

Music can be a gift, recording is much more of a skill. Give yourself time, try reading the manuals, and just try things out. Not everyone can be a star, I should know, I've been doing this stuff for 20 years and the most I've made out of my music so far was 25 quid that was spent on a well deserved curry. That said, I am about to release my first album of music, written, created, recorded, mixed and produced all on my PC using the software mentioned in these pages (check it out on http://www.moltenmeditation.com). It is completely possible to do this. But really, that's not the point. I make music because it gives me pleasure and I will continue to do so as long as it does.

Give it a go.

The later chapters of this book deal with PC music in more practical terms – showing you how to handle Windows, suggesting ways of setting up your studio (term used very loosely), and lists of products and contacts to give you an idea of what's actually out there to buy.

# Tackling Windows XP

**H** aving a basic grasp of the media functions within Windows XP is pretty essential to the overall PC music making experience.

Operating systems change and evolve, and each new update seems to bring new headaches for the computer musician. We just want something clean, fast and compatible. The best way to make an OS really stable is to make it incompatible with anything remotely interesting – and so we have Linux and Unix.

**Figure 11.1**
Windows XP Logo.

Windows Vista (scheduled for release in 2007) promises (they always 'promise') lots of music orientated features as well as fantastic stability and performance. Unfortunately it's unlikely to be compatible with much as your recording software or soundcard drivers may well have to be re-written to work directly with it. This will happen, but don't expect it to happen overnight. Give it at least 6 months before pouncing on a new OS – let the music manufacturers try it out, iron out the bugs and get it all working before getting on the bandwagon. For now Windows XP (Home or Professional) still holds the mantle as the best OS for music, we like it, know it intimately and can get all sorts of things to work on it. If you want to take advantage of everything that a 64 bit system has to offer then you can use Windows XP x64 Edition but first make sure that the software you want to use and the soundcard you need to work with it are 64 bit compatible.

**Figure 11.2**
Windows Vista on the horizon.

## Optimisation

Before we check out the audio ins and outs of Windows let's give it a bit of a tune up and see if we can get it running at its optimum for music production. General use of a PC like office work, internet browsing, gaming and mucking about will, over time, clog the system up with all sorts of things that you probably don't need or are even aware of.

Take a glance at your clock in the bottom right corner of the screen, in what is called the 'System Tray'. Do you see all those icons? If there's a 'Hide inactive icons' arrow then click it to reveal the full horror. Each of these innocent looking graphics hides a greedy and jealous heart. They represent a program or a service that's running on your computer and each one requires a bite of your CPU's processing pie. Some of these icons are regular Windows things like network connections, volume controls but most of them get installed when you install other software. Some have their own settings that enable it to run in the background. Microsoft Messenger (MSM) is a good example. If you open Messenger, which will probably be sitting next to the clock, and go to the 'Tools' menu and then 'Options' and then 'Preferences' you can uncheck the boxes next to 'Run when Windows starts' and 'Allow to run in background'. Click 'OK' and close the program and Messenger will no longer appear in the system tray. You can look at the other icons and many of them will be able to let you turn them off.

**Figure 11.3**
An unhelpful amount of system tray icons.

Now there is a more aggressive way of dealing with this and it can also unearth a bunch of other services that are running hidden away, without the politeness of a little icon to announce its presence. We're going to look at the System Configuration Utility.

Hold down the Windows key on your keyboard and press 'R' and the 'Run' window appears (keyboard shortcuts are very handy and always impress). Now type 'msconfig' (without the quotes) and the System Configuration Utility will appear. All we're interested in is the 'Startup' tab, so click it and have a look at the list shown there.

All of the items listed run when your system starts up. Some of them will have a corresponding icon in the System Tray but many will not. Now they are not all bad, one may refer to your soundcards volume or control panel, another to your graphics card drivers, but the vast majority can be deselected. Classic annoying services are things like Apple's 'iTunes Helper' (who needs help with that?), Quicktime, Realsched, Adobe Acrobat updater and the Nero update utility, none of which needs to be running in the background of Windows. In fact it's probably best to 'disable all' of them and see what happens. Click 'OK' and restart your system when prompted.

**Figure 11.4**
The System Configuration Utility shows you what runs on startup – disable them!

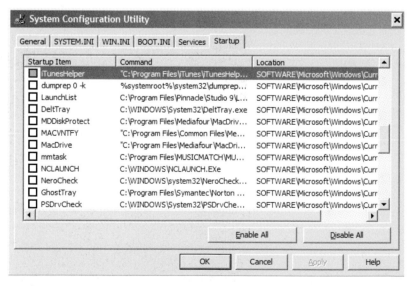

If there was a lot to disable then the first thing you should notice is how blisteringly fast Windows booted up – from the 'Welcome' to the desktop in no time at all. Then you'll see a warning telling you what you've done. Check the 'Don't show me again' box and close the window. Now look at your clock, hopefully much less crowded down there. Start your usual programs and make sure it all works. If you get any errors on startup then you may have something connected that requires a driver or service that you've now disabled. Go back into the System Configuration Utility and enable it. If you look at the 'Command' line next to each item you can usually see where they come from and what they refer to.

You should find your system feels much less clunky, a bit more speedy and less likely to give you glitches in your audio work. If you install any new software or hardware check to see if any new icons appear in the System Tray and routinely check the System Configuration Utility for those sneaky, power sucking little gremlins.

Other things to disable while working with music would be virus checkers, desktop themes, screensavers, networks, email, in fact disconnect from the internet all together.

## Music in Windows XP

The best place to start is the fully integrated Media Player which you should find located right under the 'Start' menu.

With a bit of luck the Media Player will launch into the last thing you had playing. If not, hit the 'Play' button or find an audio file in the 'Media Library' that will list all compatible files on your system. You should now be hearing whatever audio file you selected, if you click on the 'Now Playing' tab you'll be able to see what file is playing. If you are not getting any sound at all then it will be one of or more of the following four things:

Figure 11.5
Microsoft Media Player version 11 is well worth the download if you don't have it already. It's free and brings stacks of extra features including direct streaming from online shops.

- You don't have a soundcard – hopefully we would have established this by now.
- You haven't connected your speakers – in all the years I've been doing tech support this is one of the most common problems people have. Check your cables, make sure the right plugs are in the right socket – if in doubt try it in all the holes until it works.
- The Windows volume controls are down or muted – we'll come to that in a minute.
- Your soundcard isn't installed correctly – we'll tackle that after the volume bit.

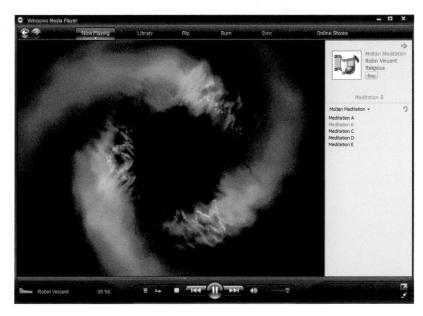

## Volume control

This is staggeringly important and the cause of so much unnecessary frustration and technical support. Windows has a volume control which controls the input and output (recording and playback) levels of your soundcard. The software that came with your soundcard may contain a flashy mixer in which case use that and consult your documentation, but the concepts are the same as using the default Windows volume controls.

So where are they? Well, you'll often find a shortcut to the volume controls through a little speaker icon next to the clock, if not then try from the Start menu under Accessories – Entertainment. It should look something like this: (the number of channels displayed will be dependent upon the capabilities of your soundcard and what channels have been selected to be shown).

**Figure 11.6**
Windows volume controls.

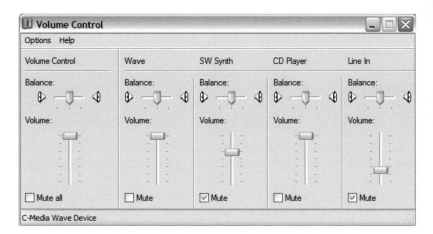

- Volume Control – overall volume control of everything.
- Wave – this is the audio volume control. Audio files are known as 'wave' files.
- SW Synth – this is for the Microsoft GS Soft Synth.
- CD Player – the volume of audio CD playback.
- Line In – this controls the input level through the line input socket, it's not really volume as such, but a recording control.

If you didn't hear anything when using the Media Player, check the relevant levels. In my volume control panel you can see that the SW Synth channel is muted out and the level is quite low. If I tried to play back a MIDI file I would hear nothing at all. So in order to remedy this I need to deselect 'mute' and raise the level.

Click on 'options' and select 'properties'. This dialogue box allows you to choose which volume controls you want to see and whether you want playback or recording controls.

## Recording controls

We'll take a quick look at the recording controls, so select them and press 'OK'. You'll usually see at least Line-in and Microphone. By checking the box on a channel it allows your soundcard to record audio through that input. So, if you plugged a microphone into your soundcard you should select the Microphone channel or you will be recording nothing.

Figure 11.7
Windows recording controls.

Let's have a quick go at recording something. Either plug the microphone that came with your soundcard into the mic input, or if you can play CDs through your soundcard then stick in an audio CD. Make sure you have selected the correct input channel in the recording control panel.

No real improvements have been made to the old Sound Recorder since Windows 3.1, still, it seems to do the very basic job of recording which is all we need for now. You'll find the 'Sound Recorder' under the Start menu Accessories – Entertainment. Speak into your microphone or play the CD and you should see lines of green blobs appearing in the sound recorder window as in Figure 11.12. If not then check the recording input selection again. With any luck you'll be hard disk recording. If not, read on.

Figure 11.8
Windows Sound Recorder.

## Sound management within Windows XP

So how does Windows XP relate to your soundcard and other music making devices attached to your PC? To see what's going on you need to delve into the 'Control Panel''. You'll find it under the 'Start' menu. Once it's open click the 'Switch to Classic view' button to get to the nitty gritty of the system.

There are two icons that we are interested in here, 'Sounds and Audio Devices' and 'System'. 'Sounds and Audio Devices' is where all the sound and music facilities for normal Windows operation are configured (professional soundcards may have their own control panels as well). 'System' shows you where devices are installed and allows you to resolve any conflicts that arise when you install a new bit of hardware.

**Figure 11.9**
Windows Control Panel.

## Sounds and audio devices

Double clicking this icon will bring up the sound properties window. The parts
we are interested in are 'Audio' and 'Hardware'.

### Audio window

The Audio window displays the default sound recording, playback and MIDI
settings for the computer. I suppose this is only useful if you have more than
one 'sound' device in your system, but then all sorts of things have audio
drivers like modems, bluetooth and video capture cards but they are generally a really bad idea for music. You need to select the device that refers to
your soundcard. Sometimes the actual name of the device is something
strange, like the name of the audio chipset. Here I'm using the on-board
soundcard called 'C-Media' and so I've selected it as the default playback
device. This is for general windows sounds and games/multimedia playback.
For recording I've chosen a much higher quality soundcard called the Delta
44 from M-Audio that would give me a much better recording result than the
on-board soundcard. In most music software you get the option to select
sound devices directly, so this window is only really setting defaults for
Windows sounds – such as Media Player. The default MIDI synth, which
Media Player would use for playing back MIDI files, is the now infamous
Microsoft GS Wavetable Soft Synth.

Clicking the 'Advanced' button opens a window where you can set up different speaker configurations (if your card supports it) but you can also
change a couple of performance characteristics. Set the sample rate to 'best'

quality, unfortunately XP doesn't allow us to specify a sample rate. This would have to be done in the soundcard's own software. 'Hardware acceleration'? Yes please.

## Hardware window

The Hardware window shows a list of media devices installed in your system and gives you access to a few properties such as enable/disable, installation and driver details. In the example in Figure 11.11 I have a number of entries which I will try to explain.

### Sony CD-RW

This is a hardware CD and DVD player/recorder. I can set volume levels, change DVD region and check the drivers.

### Unimodem Half Duplex Audio Device

This is the audio input for the installed modem – the device you would use with a handset.

### E-MU E-DSP Audio Processor (WDM)

This is the audio driver for the Emu 0404 soundcard installed in my computer. It's a high quality music card with an on-board DSP chip for effects.

### C-Media AC97 Audio Device

This is the entry for the on-board soundcard provided by C-Media and complies with the AC97 standard for multimedia.

### Audio codecs

A 'codec' is a compression/decompression technology. Audio codecs are software interpreters for different audio formats, audio streams and compression formats. All installed codecs will be listed here. For example there would be a codec for wave file playback, another for MP3 playback.

### Legacy audio drivers

These allow compatibility with older Windows audio formats.

There are others but that's the main gist of things. Your list may look somewhat different but it should give you an idea about what they refer to.

## System

Let's go back to the Control Panel and double click the 'System' icon to have a quick look at where the soundcards are installed relative to the rest of the computer.

**Figure 11.10**
Windows audio window.

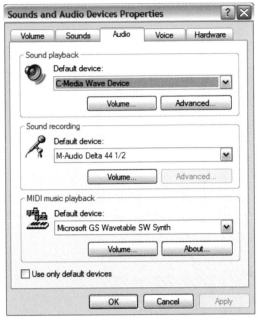

**Figure 11.11**
Windows hardware window.

To reach the Device Manager (Figure 11.12) you need to click on the 'Hardware' tab and then the 'Device Manager' button. Your soundcard devices can be found under 'Sound, video and game controllers'. This list is essentially identical to the one we found in the Hardware window. The Device Manager also lists everything else installed in your computer and shows you what resources everything is using. Using the 'View' menu you can also see what IRQ's (Interrupt Requests) devices are using which is useful when installing new hardware. Windows XP goes a long way to prevent you from messing with the settings, but it's also very good at organising things intelligently which should mean that you don't need to look in here at all – which is nice. This is also where you can uninstall/reinstall drivers if problems occur, or update drivers to newer versions as they become available.

**Figure 11.12**
The Device Manager in Windows lists everything installed on your computer.

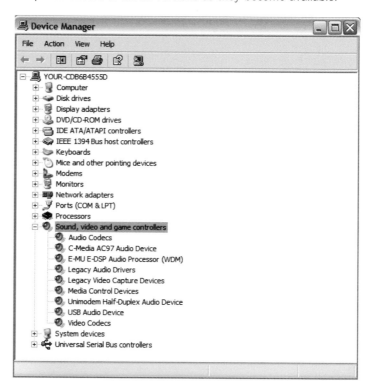

### Further optimisation of Windows XP

Following the 'Optimisation' guidelines from the beginning of this chapter should be enough for most people and most applications. However, if you really want to squeeze out every drop from your system then let's look at what else can be done to optimise Windows XP for audio.

Open the 'System' window again and this time go to 'Advanced'. Under 'Performance' click the settings button. Now take off all the visual effects. Yes I know we like to see windows fade in and out and slide about, but it's taking up valuable resources, so it's got to stop. Click on the 'Advanced' tab and you'll find a setting for virtual memory. There are many schools of thought about the actual amount of virtual memory that should be set. As far as I can see it's only really important to have it set to the same value for minimum and maximum values, that way Windows will never try to resize the virtual memory swap file right in the middle of a massive mixdown. A good rough figure would be twice your physical RAM. Also on the 'Advanced' tab is 'Processor Scheduling' which is probably set to 'Programs'. Change this to 'Background Services' and windows will give priority to your soundcard drivers, meaning that there will be less chance of glitching in your audio playback.

## Summary

That should give you a good idea about what's going on in Windows XP and with a bit of luck your system will be running nice and smoothly, ready for you to start punishing it with your music.

# PC music setups

This is probably what you really want to see – how to set it all up. The problem from my point of view is that it really does depend on what you've got and what you are trying to do. I get many emails from people saying they have this, that and three of these and how on earth do they plug it all together? My reply to which is often 'I don't know, how do you want to plug it together?' I'm not trying to be funny but this does all come down to what you want to do. For instance, if you have a hardware mixer and hardware effects then you plug it together in such a fashion as to make it do what you want it to do – it can be the same with computer music gear. That said there are some basic rules you can follow and what you need to do is try to apply what I'm showing you to your own gear. Most importantly, if you don't know why you need something then you probably don't need it. Mixers are a classic example. The number of people I've heard from who bought mixers because someone said they needed one but have no idea what it is or how to use it. You only need a mixer if you know you need a mixer, if you're not sure then the likelihood is that you do not need one. The best way to decide whether you need a mixer is to count up how many boxes you have that make a noise. If it's just your PC then you don't need a mixer. If you've got racks of hardware synths and a Korg Trinity keyboard then you are going to want to 'mix' all those sounds together so that they come out of the same pair of speakers – then you need a mixer. Even then, if you get a soundcard with lots of inputs then your external gear can be piped into the computer as well and mixed on screen. If you have one knocking about, they can be useful, but if you don't then you probably don't need one.

So, how do you plug it all in? Here are a couple of examples of ways you could connect up a computer based home or project studio including using a mixer. Remember it does all depend on what gear you've got and if you haven't got anything then the purchase of the right soundcard or audio interface will make setting up your system very easy.

## Your first studio

To make music on your computer you need a soundcard. Most computers come with a rubbish one built in that gives you a mic input, a line input and line or speaker outputs. Now don't go thinking just because you've got built in 7.1 surround with some kind of high definition Sound Blaster chipset that it's going to be any good for making music – it'll do for starters but you may discover that it has many frustrating limitations and if you make the jump to a soundcard that's designed for music production your computer music making experience will vastly improve. Anyway, check out the Chapter 6 on soundcards for more on that, let's get on with dealing with what we find.

One PC, built-in soundcard, one MIDI keyboard (optional), a guitar (optional – could be a microphone) and a pair of speakers (these could potentially be headphones) – groovy.

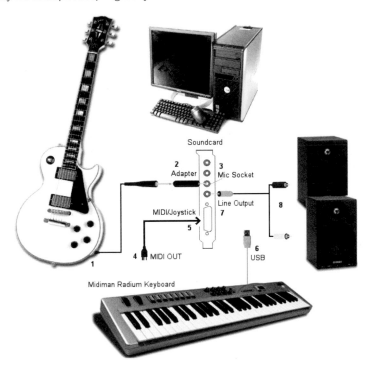

Figure 12.1
Your basic home studio.

Okay, let's have a go at explaining what's going on by numbers.

1  Plug a guitar cable into your guitar. The guitar is being used here as an example of an instrument. It could be any other instrument or just a microphone.
2  The standard soundcard has mini-jack inputs so you need to use an adapter to take your guitar cable jack (1/4 inch) down to a mini-jack (3.5mm).
3  Plug the adapted cable into the microphone socket on the soundcard.
4  MIDI keyboards often now come with a USB socket, if yours does, go to number 6. If not then take a MIDI cable and plug it into the MIDI OUT on the keyboard.
5  Using a MIDI/joystick adapter plug the other end of the MIDI cable into the joystick port. Remember that you only need this if your MIDI keyboard does not have a USB port.
6  A MIDI keyboard with a USB socket is providing its own MIDI interface to the computer. Just plug the USB cable from the keyboard into the USB

port on the computer, install the driver, and the keyboard is ready to go.

7 Line output on the soundcard is also a mini-jack, so you'll need a cable with stereo mini-jack on one end and whatever your speakers need on the other.

8 The Line output goes to your powered speakers, one left, one right. If you have passive speakers then plug the Line Output into the amp that's powering the speakers.

Your recording software will be able to record the guitar, and the keyboard will be able to play software synths. All the sound, from the guitar and the soft synths will come out of the Line Output into your speakers.

See, that was easy! Audio cabling is very simple and you can adapt any analogue audio connector to any other – small jack to big jack, phono to XLR, bare speaker wire into jacks – whatever you like. All decent electrical or hi-fi stores should have a range.

Ideally, you shouldn't connect a guitar into a mic socket, you should use a preamp and then into the Line Input or your soundcard should have a proper instrument input. Before we look at what a setup using a proper professional audio interface looks like let's see if we can use that old mixer.

## Using a mixer

As I've already said you don't need a mixer unless you know you need one, however, it's one of the most common questions I get asked so here's an example of how to use a small mixer, this could even be an old 4-track recorder, with your computer. What the mixer does supply is a decent input stage for mics and instruments rather than using the little mic input on an inbuilt soundcard.

Let's use a better, but simple, recording soundcard called the Audiophile from M-Audio with high quality inputs, one MIDI synth keyboard with its own sounds (this is why we need a mixer – we have external sounds we want to 'mix' in), a guitar, a mic and a pair of speakers. Let's see if you can follow this one (Figure 12.2).

1 Plug a guitar cable into your guitar.

2 Plug a suitable cable into your microphone.

3 Plug the mic and guitar into separate channels on the mixer. You could use a separate preamp for the guitar and the microphone if you like.

4 The keyboard has both a MIDI OUT and IN, this is so we can send MIDI OUT to the computer for recording, and then receive the MIDI back IN from the sequencer so the synth plays the sounds (eg. drums and instrument backing). This assumes your keyboard has its own sounds that you want to use, if not then you just need the MIDI OUT.

5 The Audiophile's MIDI interface provides the MIDI IN and OUT sockets. Remember that the OUT from the keyboard goes to the IN on the interface and vice versa. If the keyboard has a USB port then you could use that instead of the MIDI interface.

6 We want to be able to hear the synth, so we plug the audio output into the mixer.

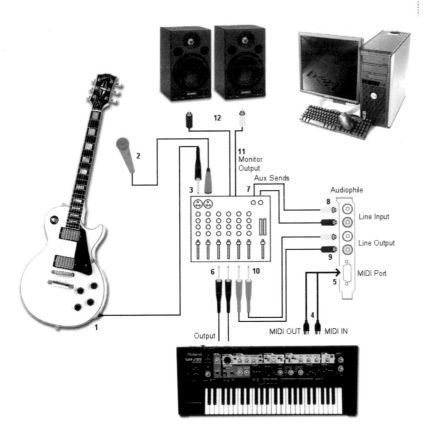

Figure 12.2
A setup incorporating a mixer.

7  This is the bit people usually have trouble with. We want to be able to record the mic and guitar onto the computer. If we used the mixer's master outputs then while we are recording the guitar we would record the backing from the synth at the same time onto the same track. We don't want to do this, we want to record everything onto different tracks, and we don't want to record the synth until we're completely sure of the MIDI arrangement in the software (you still with me?). So, we need to SEND the guitar and the mic to the soundcard separately. How do we do this? We use SENDS. All mixers have an auxiliary send or two, sometimes called 'FX Sends' as that's what they are normally used for – sending the signal from channels out to effects. However, this time we are going to use them like an output, and send the guitar/mic channel out of the send and to the soundcard. So, turn up the send knob on the guitar and mic channels, and make sure the sends on the other channels are at zero. Now we'll be able to hear the synth, but it won't get recorded with the guitar. Super, got that? Good.

8  The output from the aux send, ideally two for stereo, is plugged into the Line Input on the Audiophile (soundcard).

9  Now, we want to be able to hear the recorded guitar at the same time as the output of the hardware synth, so the Line Output of the Audiophile needs to be plugged into the mixer.

10 Make sure the aux send on the channels for the soundcards output are at zero or you might get feedback through the computer.

11 The monitor output of the mixer carries the recorded tracks from the computer and the output of the synth and should be plugged into your speakers.

12 All the sound comes out of your powered speakers, or amp and speaker arrangement.

A good note to make at this point is that although you're using a mixer, you're not actually using it to mix anything. All you've got is a stereo output from the synth, possibly carrying multiple tracks of different instruments and the stereo output from the computer, which could carry a couple of guitars, vocals and harmony. So, all the mixing needs to be done on the computer, in Cubase or whatever you're using. Also if your mixer has direct outputs, tape outputs or busses then you don't need to use the auxiliaries, just treat the computer like a hardware recorder.

## Recording a band

If you make the leap to a proper audio interface for recording then suddenly the possibilities really start opening up. In this example I'm going to use the excellent Firepod from Presonus. It's a firewire interface providing 8 mic or line inputs on the front and several other connections on the back. The are a number of other audio interfaces available with similar connections up to a total of 96 inputs (the most I've seen so far) when you stack a few of them together. You can run two or three Firepods together if you need 16 or 24 inputs. Let's keep it simple for the moment and show how versatile 8 inputs can be and hopefully demonstrate the reality of what can be plugged directly into a computer for recording.

As you can see (Figure 12.3) you don't need a mixer. The Firepod is providing all the inputs and preamps you need, for mics, for guitars, for whatever you want to throw at it. All the mixing is done on the computer in your audio software resulting in a stereo monitor output going to your speakers. If you are unhappy about the idea of mixing with a mouse then you'll need to enter the world of the MIDI control surface where you have a slab of plastic with a bunch of faders and knobs that you use to control the software mixer on screen – full tactile control often with motorised faders and all sorts of flashing lights.

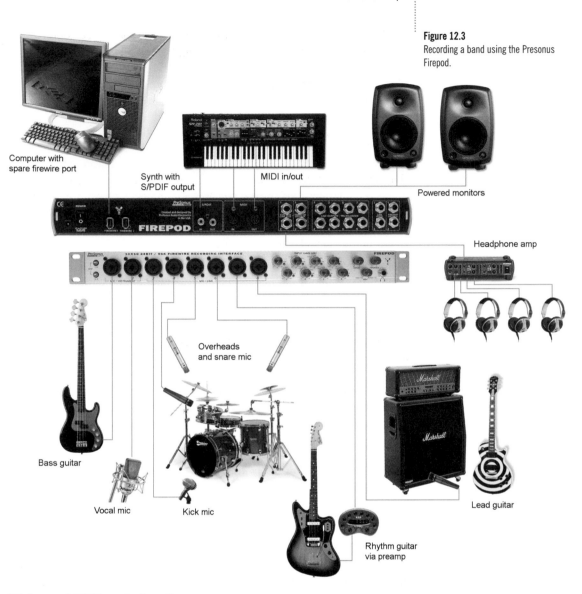

**Figure 12.3**
Recording a band using the Presonus Firepod.

Computer with spare firewire port

Synth with S/PDIF output

MIDI in/out

Powered monitors

Headphone amp

Overheads and snare mic

Bass guitar

Vocal mic

Kick mic

Lead guitar

Rhythm guitar via preamp

## Mixing and MIDI control surfaces

If you are used to the traditional studio setup, using analogue gear, mixers and faders and the like then you may have some trouble getting your head around the idea that everything is now controlled by the mouse. Don't worry, it's a common quandary and one that is easily relieved thanks to the array of MIDI control surfaces that are available. I've mentioned MIDI control in some of the other chapters but I thought it would be particularly relevant here. On screen in programs like Cubase you have a wonderful, glowing and pulsating mixer, all automated, in movement, like some kind of dance.

That's all well and good but what if you want to make quick fader adjustments in more places than one at a time, or want to 'ride' some faders on playback, or bring up a whole section as you feel it happening rather than having to write it all in beforehand with a mouse? Well, let's wheel in the

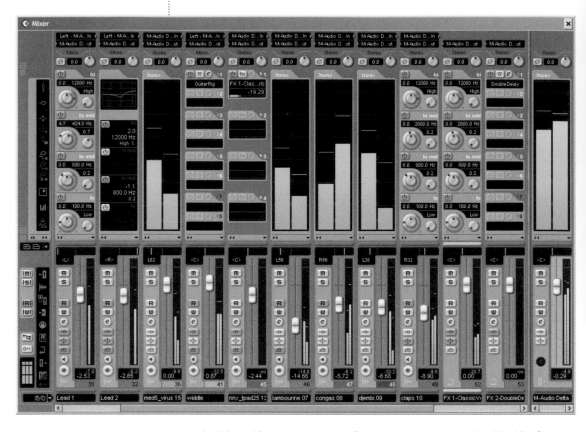

**Figure 12.4**
Cubase Mixer.

standard by which all control surfaces are measured – the Mackie Control. Your standard Mackie Control 'Universal' comes with eight 100mm motorized 'flying' track faders and one master fader each with a rotary V-Pot assignable to any parameter. Dedicated record arm, mute, solo and channel select buttons and an LED display showing exactly what you're controlling. Full navigation control is given with transport buttons and a jog/scrub wheel. You can switch the eight faders to cover channel 9-16, 17-24 etc with the touch of a button – all settings memorized and returned to on the fly. Eight

**Figure 12.5**
Mackie Control

faders not enough? Then bolt on another eight with the Mackie Expander. You really don't need to use a mouse at all when mixing with the Mackie Control.

There are many other surfaces available. Some, like the Digi002 or Tascam FW1884 combine a control surface with the soundcard giving you what essentially is a digital mixer directly into the computer with the added bonus of full software control.

If all this looking a bit professional and therefore expensive then you will be happy to find that there are plenty of cheaper options. Many MIDI keyboards now come with faders and knobs attached to give you some mixing control or maybe control over software synth parameters. The Korg Kontrol 49 is a good and classy example. It's a 4 octave keyboard with full size keys, 8 faders, 8 rotary knobs and 16 pads, like those you'd find on a drum machine.

**Figure 12.6**
Korg Kontrol 49.

Or for the coolest budget gear check out Behringer as they cannot be beaten on quality with value.

Can you find any other reasons not to move to a computer based recording studio?

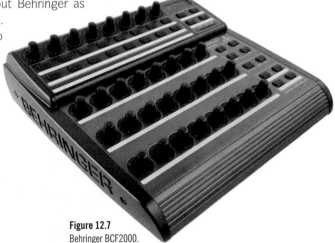

**Figure 12.7**
Behringer BCF2000.

# The dance music appendium

**C**omputers and modern electronic dance music go hand in hand, they are inseparable and obvious bedfellows. In fact many people believe that this is the only use of computers in music. Hopefully I've shown you otherwise. In writing this book I have avoided being genre or style specific, simply because everything I have talked about is applicable to any sort of music, but I think it would be good to take a look at the sort of tools used on computer to generate dance, electronic, house, techno, trance, acid, jungle, drum 'n' bass, ambient or whatever it is you want to call it (I'll refer to it as 'dance' for simplicity).

The beauty of dance music is that it doesn't necessarily require any musical training or ability to play an instrument. Anyone can do it (not to say that there are not plenty of very learned music professionals involved in making dance music). The friendly user interface and robotic timing of the computer has brought 'banging beats' to the masses. The music isn't necessarily played into the computer but rather programmed with the use of mouse. A favourite way of entering notes is using the piano-roll editor or, even better, the drum grid if your sequencer has one. You could look at a four bar loop, overlay a grid of 16 beats and put a closed hi-hat on every line. Follow that with a bass drum on every 4th, and an open hi-hat on the off beat (2nd, 6th, 10th and 14th) and you have a classic dance music drum pattern. If you find this a little uninspiring and really can't seem to come up with the pattern you're after then there are a range of drum pattern MIDI files available on disk. Simply open the file and copy-and-paste the patterns into your song. How easy is that? Mind you, if you're going to let someone else do all the music for you, you may as well pack it in and put on a CD! But it's a start and it may give you some ideas.

You can make dance music with anything. You could knock out some beats with a tin can and a stick if you like, but there are some common tools of the trade that no self respecting dance musician/programmer should be without.

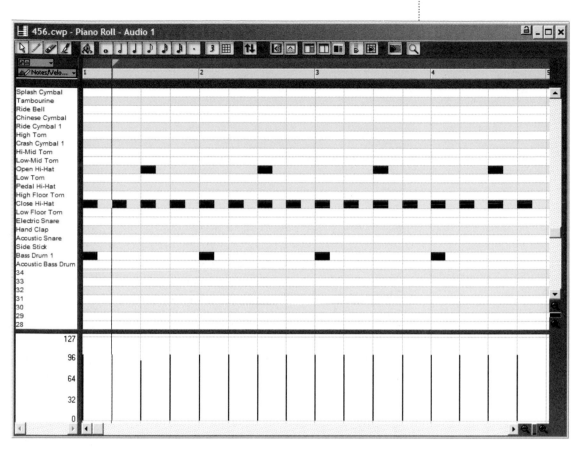

## Sampler

Quick recap – a sampler is a device that holds a piece of audio which is triggered for playback via MIDI.

Why do you need a sampler? There are three main uses of samplers in dance music:

The drum sounds – with a sampler you can copy a drum sound from another piece of music and use it in your own song, or you can buy a Sample CD that has drum sounds already sampled for you. The exact same thing can be done with loops and hits.

Rather than programming your own patterns and phrases you can simply trigger loops and hits from your sequencer. People have been doing a similar sort of thing with twin record decks for years.

The computer can make another useful appearance here as a sample editor. You can use software like Sony's Sound Forge or Steinberg's Wavelab to edit samples and then dump them back to the sampler. Editing may include the removal of noise, trimming the sample so it's the right length for looping, trimming the start of the sample, adding effects or just generally mucking about with them.

A terribly useful piece of software is Propellerhead's Recycle. It does the relatively simple job of cutting up a loop into its component parts and arrang-

**Figure 13.1**
A classic 'dance music' drum pattern

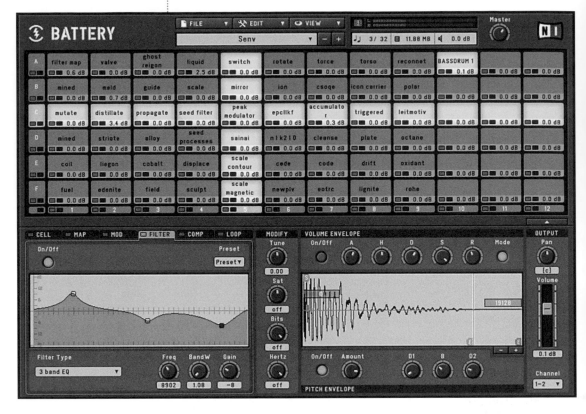

**Figure 13.2**
Native Instruments Battery drum sampler.

ing the now individual samples across a keyboard like a drum kit. Anyone who's tried doing this in a hardware sampler will tell you that it can take hours to do it by hand.

## Hardware or software sampler?

With the power of software like GigaStudio, Halion or Kontakt you can match the facilities of a hardware sampler and do a lot of other stuff their hardware colleagues cannot. You have all the editing and the sequencing on the same machine, masses of hard disk space to store samples and for a few hundred quid less than a hardware sampler. There are some advantages to hardware samplers but these are mostly to do with the immediacy and physicality of it rather than any particular features.

**Figure 13.3**
Akai's MPC2000XL a real hands-on hardware sampler.

# Filters

One of the more obvious tools is the filter, well, obvious once you know what it is. You would have heard the effect a hundred times usually on a synth bass sound, often applied to drums, sometimes used on anything and everything. To describe the effect of a filter in words is very difficult (I've been trying to do this for hours) and the best I can come up with is to say it makes a kind of a sweeping 'psshhhoowaaaaarrrh' sound. Hmmm, perhaps it's better to describe what a filter actually does and then you might be able to spot the effect yourself.

There are many types of filters including 6 pole, 4 pole, 2 pole, resonant, hi-pass, band-pass, low-pass, comb, to name a few. EQ or equalisation is also a form of filtering. A filter does as the name suggests, it removes, or 'filters', a specified frequency range of an audio signal. A very common one is the low-pass filter. This allows (or passes) low frequencies through unchanged up to a specified frequency. All frequencies above this 'cut-off' point are blocked. So, if you slowly increase the cut-off from zero to fully open you'll hear the gradual inclusion of higher frequencies in the sound giving a tonal raising in pitch effect.

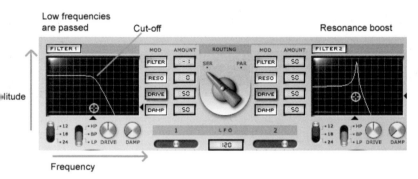

**Figure 13.4**
Two filters from TC Electronic's Filtroid. The left one showing a standard low pass filter, the right one showing the same with a resonance boost.

Resonant filters are what we are more interested in as they have a special quality of boosting the frequencies at the cut-off point. The amount of boost given to frequencies at this point and the bandwidth is called 'resonance'. The 'cut-off' and 'resonance' controls are two of the most overused in dance music.

Most software synths come with filters built in that you can mess with and you can even record and automate all the changes to get that sweeping sound over time. Filtering plug-ins are available so that you could apply it to an audio track in your hard disk recording software. For an instant idea of what this all sounds like download Propellerhead's Rebirth and you'll find a resonance and cut-off knob on both the TB303's. In fact if you haven't downloaded Rebirth yet then you have no business reading this chapter! http://www.rebirthmuseum.com/

# Analogue synths

Filters were utilised to full effect in analogue synthesis and the sounds have lent themselves to dance music. Fat bass lines, squelchy sounds, ethereal pads, and pure sounding leads come from the guts of analogue synths. The sounds are dirty, raw, warm and very broad in terms of dynamics and frequency, they just sound great.

The biggest problem is that external analogue synths (or digital 'virtual' analogue synths, which aren't bad) are quite expensive. Or, if you can find the original old style synths, they are often in bad repair and rubbish at keeping in tune. The easiest solution for us computer musicians is to get a software synth or two. The majority of software synths are angled towards recreating analogue sounds and there are tons available, all of which sound pretty good. If you have just a little bit of cash to invest you can get some amazing sounds, whole synthesisers, running on your PC – fantastic! Check out Arturia (http://www.arturia.com) and GMedia Music (http://www.gmediamusic.com) for some of the best software analogue synths around.

**Figure 13.5**
Gmedia's ImpOSCar synthesiser.

### Sequencer

This would be a good idea. The standard has been Cubase for many years for its ease of use and drum grid editor, but you can do the same stuff with Sonar, or any other sequencer. One program that should be up for real consideration by the dance musician is Reason from Propellerhead. It contains all the vital features I've just talked about, samplers, analogue synths, filters and sequencing, all in one integrated package. It doesn't come much easier than that.

One other program to consider is Ableton Live. It has a slightly different take on the whole sequencing game and uses some very clever technology to match up beats and loops and allow you to trigger them in groups. You could set up a bunch of loops for each part of your song, intro, verse, chorus etc and then trigger each section with a keystroke – it's always in time and dead easy to use. Lots of DJ's have started using programs like Live and Reason within their sets to give them a whole new performance angle.

There's also been a shareware program knocking around for years that many people swear by as the best way to create cool loops, beats and tunes.

It was called Fruity Loops and has now evolved into FL Studio. It's still a bargain and a great source of sounds and ideas.

Figure 13.6
FL Studio – get the demo and try it out.

## The rest

There are loads of bits of software out there that will help you create dance music. Lots of them are simple sample based programs or instant 'techno' machines like Rebirth. These can be a lot of fun but if you want to start creating your own stuff then it's worth looking into sampling more than anything else. There are ways around buying a sampler, you can do a lot of sample based work in your hard disk recording/sequencer program. You can import a loop and copy-and-paste along the timeline. You can cut it up and create patterns by pasting the different parts of the loop on the arrange page. You can easily add hits by simply pasting them where you want them. This is all very time consuming though and can take a lot of fiddling to get it right.
Dance music – it's fun, it's easy, it's loopy and like all other styles of music, you can create absolute rubbish, but in a much shorter time. Don't forget that a sprinkling of talent can go a long way.

# 14 The guitarist's appendium

G uitarists are simple folk (I should know, I am one), they know what they want and they don't like too much fuss. They just want to record the guitar, maybe some bass and a bit of drums, maybe even a vocal line. The most important thing is good quality, a broad dynamic sound, clear and precise, is that too much to ask? Not at all; let's look at some of the tools that will help the guitarists among you achieve the sound you're after.

## Getting the guitar into the computer

We're back to the original question about where to plug your guitar in. The traditional way of recording guitar is either to mic up the amplifier cabinet or use a guitar pre-amp and then go through a mixer.

Recording at home you are never likely to have the amp loud enough to get the sound you want, unless you live a hundred miles from your nearest neighbours.

A pre-amp, probably a better option, is a little amplifier in a box that raises the impedance of the guitar signal up to that of a line signal. This done, the output can be plugged directly into the Line-in on the soundcard and you'll get a much better recorded sound. Pre-amps come in several shapes and sizes and you may not be aware that you probably already have one. A digital effects box contains a pre-amp and this is an ideal way of getting line level into your soundcard. So plug your guitar into your effects box before the computer. You don't have to use any effects if you don't want to, it's purely providing an input stage.

A good example is the Pod from Line 6 (Figure 14.1). The Line 6 range of amplifiers contains a computer model of a number of classic amps that you can dial up depending on the type of sound you want. You want a 1960's Vox AC30 amp – no problem. They also contain effects all running at 24bit. The Pod is simply the guts of the amp version without the speaker cone. In fact all their amps have a direct out that can be plugged straight into the computer.

There are an increasing number of soundcards or audio interfaces out there that contain a guitar pre-amp built into the inputs. In fact Line 6 have a perfect solution ready to go in the Toneport.

There are two models, the UX1 and UX2 (Figure 14.2). The UX2 has 2 microphone inputs with phantom power, 2 guitar/bass inputs, stereo line inputs, mix and monitor outputs, headphones and cool assignable VU meters

**Figure 14.1**
Line 6 PODxt Ultimate tone for guitar. Models dozens of amp and cabinet combinations and over 60 effects as well as being a preamp – it also has a USB connection so you could even use it as a soundcard in it's own right.

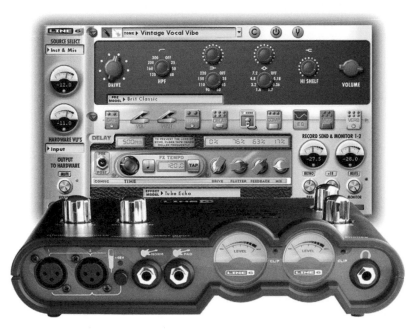

**Figure 14.2**
Line 6 Toneport UX2 – simple, gorgeous and high quality recording into the computer.

on the front. You've even got footswitch jacks for start/stop control over software – pretty nice. It all comes with the Gearbox effects and modelling software taken from the Pod giving you a stack of great guitar tones. So you've got real inputs, real knobs and meters, and it looks nothing like you'd expect a bit of computer gear to look like. It comes with some simple recording software so you can get going, and the Gearbox effects cover vocals, bass and guitar are genuinely really very good. Both units are capable of recording at 24bit and 48kHz. They connect to the PC via a USB (Universal Serial Bus) socket on the back on the computer that also provides the power. How easy is that? Guitar input, monitoring, knobs, effects and recording all in one little box with editable everything on screen. The retail is only £149 which is about the price of a decent Boss effects pedal.

There are plenty of options beyond the Toneport of increasing sound quality and features. Check out the Firepod from Presonus as an example. The

Firepod sports eight discrete mic preamps on the front, two of which can be guitar inputs all in a tasty 1U rack box. The quality is fabulous with 24bit and up to 96kHz recording. You've got mix and monitor outputs, S/PDIF and MIDI. You could you really record a whole band with this box. Not quite enough inputs for you then how about buying two and daisy chaining them together giving you 16 microphone inputs over Firewire. At around £500 it's really not that expensive.

If you feel more at home with a multitrack recorder, feeling the need for faders and the tactile studio feel of a mixer then something like the M-Audio ProjectMix I/O would fit the bill. You've got eight channel faders, a master fader, transport controls plus eight mic/line inputs, ADAT and a guitar input right on the front. You've got full control over your recording levels and full control over the software – whatever you need, however you want to work there's a solution.

**Figure 14.3**
M Audio ProjectMix I/O recording interface and surface controller.

## Software amp modelling and effects

Getting the guitar into the computer is one thing but why don't we use all that processing power to give us a load of guitar effects? Yeah, cool, there's tons of effects out there that can be used on guitar – you can play straight through them or add them later when mixing. Let's have a look at the best two:

### Native Instruments Guitar Rig 2

'Perfect custom tone' is how NI describe their versatile amp and effects 'rig'. You've got 8 amp models, 15 cabinets, 4 rotary speakers and a choice between 9 microphones so you can create your perfect combination. Then you've got 35 effects modelled on numerous legendary stomp boxes. They then chuck in a loop machine for recording and layering riffs, LFOs and step sequencers for messing about with the sound and not to mention the huge library of presets. Fabulous stuff! You may be thinking that it's a pain to have to stop playing and click a mouse to change effects but don't worry NI have also produced a floorboard controller for Guitar Rig 2 so everything is available at your feet – it can also act as your soundcard, so all you need is the Rig Kontrol and a laptop and you're good to gig.

**Figure 14.4**
Native Instruments Guitar Rig 2 a dizzying array of amps, cabinets, effects and modulators.

**Figure 14.5**
Native Instruments Rig Kontrol 2 full foot control over your software and it's also a soundcard.

## IK Multimedia Amplitube 2

'Superior Modelling, Infinite Tone' is how IK describe the successor to the award winning Amplitube. This time you've got 14 pre-amps, 7 power amps, 16 cabinets and 6 microphones to create your perfect combination from about 20,000 possible ones. Add in 21 stomp boxes based on rare and legendary guitar effects and 11 rack effects and you are in guitar noodling heaven. Hundreds of presets available on tap covering every type, every session, every possible sound you could want. IK also offer a floorboard controller but have gone further down the connectivity route with ports for expression pedals and other controllers can be patched in to give you all the control you could ever need.

**Figure 14.6**
IK Multimedia Amplitube 2 showing the amp model interface which is only part of this huge plug-in.

**Figure 14.7**
IK Multimedia's Stomp I/O hardware floorboard controller for Amplitube 2 that features a lot of connections to add further expression pedals and controllers as well as acting as a soundcard.

Phew! Both of these mammoth programs are a guitarist's paradise and will keep you plugged in for hours at a time.

## MIDI guitar synthesisers

Being a guitarist you don't necessarily play keyboards and you fancy putting some strings and synth sounds onto your songs. A good guitar synth can enable you to do this and there are MIDI pick-ups available from both Roland and Yamaha that will do a fine job. Remember, if you are using a MIDI guitar you are recording MIDI information through a MIDI interface and not actually recording the guitar sound. The sounds will come from whatever MIDI sound source you are using. Don't fall into the trap of recording guitar tracks as MIDI and wondering why the playback sound is a bit rubbish. If you want to record a guitar sound then record your actual guitar through a pre-amp or microphone.

## Recording software

Any hard disk recording program will do what you need it to so you should be looking at programs like Sonar, Cubase or Pro Tools. Cakewalk, the makers of Sonar do some guitar specific recording software which would be worth checking out – it's really good value and would a good starting point. There are also loads of guitar tuition type programs around and those that generate an automatic backing group if you just fancy having a jam.

## Drum machines

Drummers can be a right pain in your truss rod, especially when trying to write music, so the songwriter has often leant on the drum machine to provide the rhythm when composing. Boxes like the Alesis SR16 and Boss Dr Rhythm were required bits of songwriter gear. When moving to software

**Figure 14.8**
Steinberg's Groove Agent for perfect drums whatever style you're playing.

there are a number of options available to fill this roll. There are tons of sampled drums out there but most don't have any sort of patterns built in.

One notable exception is Groove Agent from Steinberg which is exactly the sort of drum machine we're talking about. It has hundreds of patterns and variations, fills and breaks, covering all sorts of styles spread across a timeline. It comes with a range of kits that you can customise, so if you want tribal techno played through a 1930's jazz kit – no problem.

Another slightly more crazy option is Jamstix from Rayzoon. It's a remarkable program because it's able to jam along with your playing. It detects your tempo and the strength you're putting into your strumming and jams along with you putting in fills and hits more or less exactly where you would have – it's a marvellous thing, go and download the demo immediately –

**Figure 14.9**
Rayzoon's Jamstix – Jam along your own virtual drummer.

http://www.rayzoon.com

Other options for instant drums is to use some of the drum loop based software instruments you can get from sample CD manufacturers such as EastWest or ZeroG – instruments packed full of drum loops that can be trigger from a keyboard. Just sequence them in and play along.

## Summary

Replacing your 4 track cassette machine with a computer and some hard disk recording software will give you power and possibilities you only dreamed of. Most guitar manufacturers have caught on to the potential of computer connections and so floorboards and preamps tend to feature USB connections more and more, enabling you to plug straight into the computer with no messing about. Guitars with USB ports built in are already upon us and Gibson's Digital Guitar shows what the future could be like if anyone can be bothered. Not all new technology is useful but if it's easy to use and gives you the sound you're after then you've got to be happy.

I recommend that once you've recorded your song you should muck around with it on screen in the arrange page. Copy and paste things around, chop things up, reverse things, and soon you'll find yourself in the exciting world of post production. Download some demos, try stuff out and don't restrict yourself to traditionally guitar based ways of doing things. It's not always rock and roll, but we like it.

**Figure 14.10**
Gibson Digital Guitar – The Ethernet
output allows for digital transmission of
the sound where, amongst other things,
each string can be treated and recorded
independently.

# The Media Center PC Appendium

W hile the PC continues to realise its potential as a music production studio it's also quietly evolving into the most extraordinary hi-fi and home theatre system. More and more off-the-shelf systems seem to ship with Windows XP Media Center edition and, with Windows Vista, 'media management' is going to be a major component.

So, what does this have to do with making music? Not a great deal, although as musicians the other thing we like to do is listen to music and with the range of musical options available to us through the internet, iTunes, Napster, podcasting, digital radio, or via digital TV and on-demand services, it would be good to take advantage of this huge wealth of material.

**Figure 15.1**
Windows XP Media Center Edition

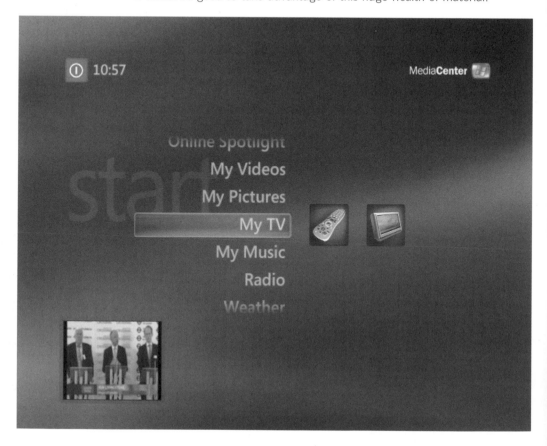

# Windows Media Center Edition

The idea behind Microsoft's Windows Media Center (MCE) is to place the PC at the centre of the home, which is, of course, beneath the living room television. Why have lots of set-top boxes and other associated bits of hardware when a single PC can fulfil the role of hi-fi, TV, DVD player, photo album, Messenger, email and internet surfing, all from the comfort of your sofa? The key to making this feasible is firstly to move away from the mouse control environment and replace it with something more TV friendly – the remote control, and secondly to create an operating system that can be run entirely from this remote. What you end up with is something not dissimilar to the menu system in Sky Digital, Cable or Freeview.

## Key ingredients

A Media Center computer would hope to contain the following:

- Windows XP Home Media Center Edition (MCE)
- MCE Remote control
- Digital TV tuner card
- Video card with TV output
- Surround sound audio output
- DVD player
- Internet connection

## Television

It's the televisual elements that really take it from being a regular PC and turn it into a media centre. TVs and PCs have never been very happy together because in comparison to a computer SVGA monitor the quality or resolution of a TV screen is rubbish. A regular TV will have up to 625 lines that make up the picture and that's the same for any size screen. A 15 inch computer screen will support 1024 lines and these are just a pixel in size. Make the screen bigger and you can pack in more lines, and so a higher resolution like 1280, 1600 and beyond. A television cannot cope with these high resolutions and so when you plug in a computer you'll find that your desktop and icons have gone very large and it's difficult to read any text. The MCE software however is designed to run at TV resolutions and so has large text, large menus and is thankfully easy to read. This is becoming less of a problem though as the prices for LCD (Liquid Crystal Display) monitors have fallen dramatically making it possible to buy large computer monitors that could replace your regular TV. High definition television (HDTV) is being developed to take advantage of the better resolution screens we are now using to give you a much better quality television picture – the programmes will be the same rubbish as usual though!

**Figure 15.2**
Windows MCE remote control.

**Figure 15.3**
All new televisions are ready for high definition broadcasts.

Currently most Media Center computers have a composite or S-Video output that translates the computer's output into a signal a regular TV can understand and with a SCART adapter it goes straight in the back. Over time these will be superseded by DVI (Digital Video Interface) outputs direct to a high resolution TV. In either case the connections are easy and Windows will detect the presence of the television and allow you to select it as the primary output.

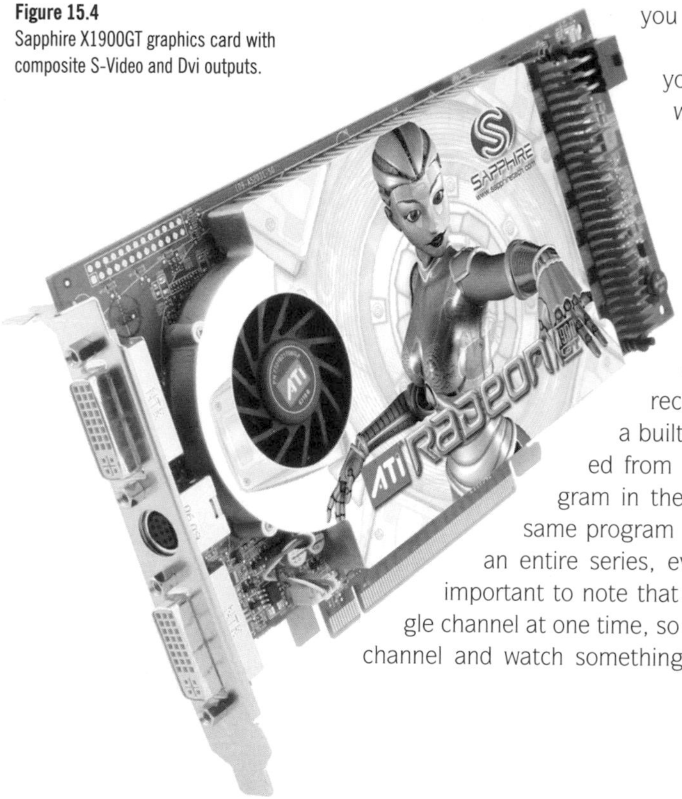

**Figure 15.4**
Sapphire X1900GT graphics card with composite S-Video and Dvi outputs.

Next up is the digital TV tuner. This allows you to connect an aerial to your PC and watch regular TV broadcasts. Tuners come with Digital Freeview built in so you have instant access to a bundle of television channels. What's really interesting though is that your PC has just become a huge video recorder. At the touch of a button on your remote you can record any program directly to hard disk. Windows MCE lets you schedule recordings up to two weeks in advance (it has a built in TV guide that gets automatically updated from the internet) by simply selecting the program in the guide. You can also set it to record the same program every time it appears and so archive away an entire series, even burn it to DVD for safe keeping. It's important to note that a single tuner can only be tuned to a single channel at one time, so if you are recording you cannot change the channel and watch something else. Thankfully dual channel tuners are

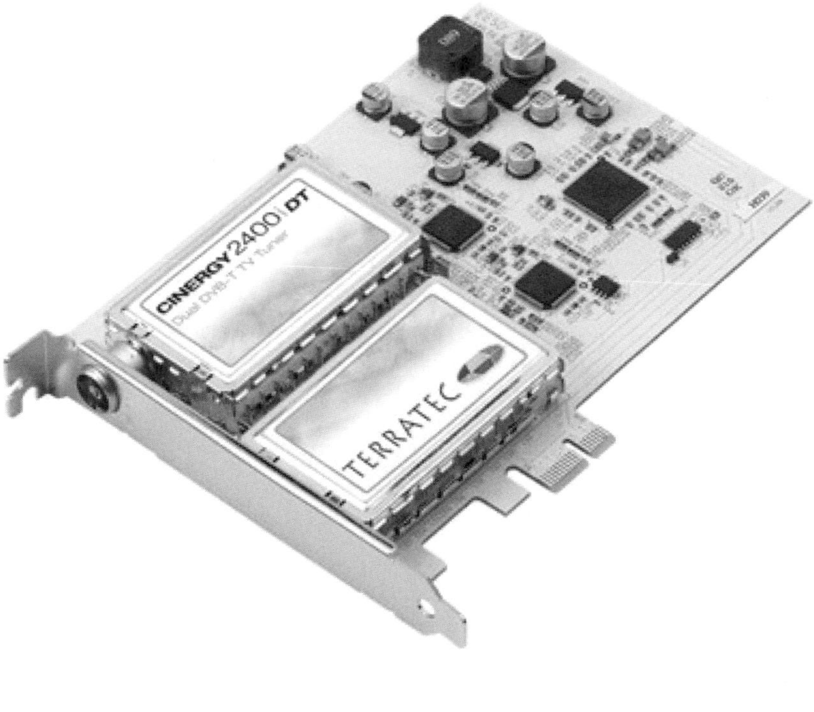

**Figure 15.5**
Terratec Cinergy 2400i DT dual tuner digital TV card.

available which allow you to watch one side while recording the other, or record two things at once. If you buy a system make sure it's got a dual channel tuner.

## Music

Windows MCE integrates Media Player and presents you with the simplest of interfaces. If you have a collection of MP3's or other media you can import it and catalogue it from the remote. Windows MCE then goes off and searches for album art and track details from the internet and you can browse your entire collection from your arm chair. You can also pull in tracks over a network so if you have another machine in your office or studio that houses your collection or your iTunes folder – no problem. With the ease of wireless networks these days it's easy to have a home network running without having to call in the experts.

Windows MCE allows for third party companies to create 'plug-ins' that will run inside the interface, Napster are one of the few that have taken them up on it. Napster subscription allows you to authorise up to three computers which is perfect for the home media centre concept. You may have Napster running on your studio computer, searching and downloading various tunes, creating playlists, and then you can run the same playlists on your living room PC. It's such a great feature.

For audio output most systems come with surround sound these days, which is of course aimed at the DVD video market but you can play music through it just as well. It may also tempt you into trying out some surround sound format DVD audio discs that are well worth it, particularly for classical music.

Windows MCE aside it's still a fully fledged computer and so you can use all the same internet driven facilities as a regular PC. One recommended purchase is the Microsoft MCE keyboard remote. It uses the same infrared interface as the hand held remote but gives you an entire QWERTY keyboard and a little thumb mouse, perfect for surfing from your sofa, getting movie trailers off Quicktime, downloading music off myspace.com and even answering your email.

If you think about it, you could be remixing some tunes in your studio (office, spare bedroom, cupboard under the stairs) and then play it back to everyone instantly in the comfort of the living room through your posh hi-fi speakers – that's really cool. Home networks also brings into mind the possibility of running software effects and instruments across multiple computers giving you increased processing power and higher track counts... Outside the scope of an 'Easy Guide' really but if you want to know more then please drop me a line.

# Products

There is loads of stuff available for turning your computer into a music making machine. The following is merely a selection of some of the more popular pieces of software and hardware currently available and is by no means definitive. If I've missed anything important then I apologise but if I haven't seen it then they can't be doing a very good job of telling people about it! Most companies also produce entry level or cut down versions of their software so if the full products seem a little pricey check out the website and you'll usually find a budget alternative.

For more in depth information on these products and others then point your browser to my companion web page which has links to manufacturers and other goodies:

http://www.pc-music.com

## Software

### Studio recording software

#### Steinberg Cubase

This is for me the complete studio package. You've got everything you need to produce music in one program. Umpteen audio and MIDI tracks, effects, mixing, automation, full support for VST Instruments and plug-ins. You've got loop editing, hit point extraction to audio quantize, you've got audio warping and tempo wrangling, online and offline processing and all wrapped up in a graphical interface that's helpful rather than cumbersome. There are two versions, SL which has everything you could need for writing and recording music, and then there's SX which includes pro scoring, surround sound mixing and some posher effects.

RRP £329 and £549. There's an entry level version called SE which is under a hundred pounds and fabulous.

http://www.steinberg.net

#### Cakewalk Sonar

Latest incarnation of Cakewalk which is the industry standard in the USA. Does loads of audio tracks with real-time FX (DirectX) processing and plenty of MIDI sequencing. Easy to use and can do everything that Cubase or pretty much any other program can do. Immensely powerful and capable. Coolest new feature in version 5 is the Roland VariPhrase plug-in that gives some amazing pitch correction on vocals and other audio tracks. Has a lot of hardware support and is a very tolerant and stable program. Always been a good program for guitarists – must be the American thing, it has a built in tuner, tab and fret board piano roll, and a session drummer.

It uses the DirectX plug-in format natively and now supports Rewire, VST plug-ins and ASIO soundcard drivers. RRP £249. PC only – born and bred. There are tons of versions, two of Sonar, Studio and Producer, and then lots of Cakewalk versions underneath.

http://www.cakewalk.com

### Digidesign Pro Tools LE

Pro Tools LE is undoubtedly an awesome recording and editing program. It's almost exactly the same software as used by recording professionals in pro studios the world over. Its big brother, Pro Tools 'HD' has support for more tracks and is integrated with hardware DSP cards that run the audio engine. The 'LE' version loses the DSP and runs purely as a host version with the computer doing all the work. This removes much of what makes Pro Tools the professional choice, however, it's still the same software with the same tools it just doesn't work quite as well as the 'HD' version, but then it's several thousand pounds cheaper! The strength of Pro Tools LE is in the audio recording and editing. It works very much like a hardware studio would, so people used to hardware would find Pro Tools LE the easiest software to get into. The MIDI side of the program has always been poor and has not been able to compete with programs like Cubase, however, new version 7 goes a long way to addressing those sorts of issues so now (finally) it's a more complete compositional package rather than just recording software. Despite this being a host based version it still requires specific hardware to run and so is not available to buy off the shelf. Pro Tools LE only comes with and will only run with Digidesign's own Digi002, 002Rack and MBox2. However, Avids (Digidesign's parent company) recent acquisition of M-Audio has produced a version called Pro Tools M-Powered which is the same as LE but runs on the M-Audio range of audio cards and interfaces. This you can buy off the shelf for £249.

http://www.digidesign.com

### Ableton Live

The idea behind this offering is to make sequencing and sample messing a more 'Live' experience. You can drop in different samples and loops in real time and mess them about, 'jam' if you will with the software. Here's how they describe it:

Live is an audio sequencer that you can play like an instrument. On your own or with other musicians or DJs, live on stage or when remixing in the studio, all you need is Live and a Mac or PC. Live allows you to bring together audio material from various sources. All the samples used are adjusted to the tempo of the song in real time without changing the pitch.

Even long pieces with tempo variations play in perfect sync. Samples can be played back and new ones can be recorded using the mouse, computer keyboard or MIDI notes. Drag-and-drop can be used to put together any sequence of effects for sound editing, without interrupting the music. Everything you do during the session is recorded and can be edited in detail afterwards, including all the automation of the mixer and effects. It includes all the usual recording facilities you'd find in other recording programs. It's

http://www.ableton.com

an amazing program, fun to play with and easy to get started with.

If you're looking for something different or you can't seem to get along with Cubase and the like then check this out. RRP £299.

### Propellerhead Reason

You'll never get the idea about Reason until you see the amazing rack of stuff that's going on. Reason is basically a huge rack of synths, samplers and effects. You've got subtractive and additive synths, wavetable and granular, you've got samplers and loop players and one of the most intuitive drum machines available. Bolt onto that a ton of effects and mixing and you've got yourself a pretty comprehensive writing tool.

You've got a built in sequencer into which you can record pattern changes or MIDI input from a keyboard. You have matrix style pattern sequencers that you can attach to any synth or sampler. Then you can flip the whole thing over and start messing about with the routing using virtual cables. You can take the output from one synth and use it as a modulator for something else or wire anything into anything else.

The one thing Reason will not do at this time is record audio, so you can't plug your guitar in and record a track, it only deals with what's contained in the program. However, through the miracle of 'Rewire' the outputs of Reason can be routed through Cubase, Sonar, Live or Pro Tools, and they turn up as another fader on the mixer. Then you can record your audio tracks and other stuff alongside.

http://www.propellerheads.se

This is one of my favourite bits of software and no self respecting computer musician should be without it. RRP £249.

### Mackie Tracktion

Written by a fellow who reckoned that all other sequencing software was rubbish and impossible to use and so he designed this to be simply easy and yet as powerful as everyone else. By all accounts he seemed to have accomplished it and I know of lots of people who have struggled with Sonar or Cubase and really love it. I would say this is a serious contender, especially for those on a budget. RRP £110.

http://www.tracktion.com

## Wave/Sample Editing

### Sony Sound Forge

Sound Forge is renowned for stability and ability to handle huge files instantly and without question. The interface is quite sparse and feels like an old school audio editor where the keyboard is king – and you do tend to fly around using the keys more than the mouse which makes it very fast to use. Recent versions now (at last) include VST plug-in support as well as DirectX although it's quite fussy and doesn't tolerate badly written plug-ins. It seems to be able to read and export to any format on the planet. CD mastering and batch processing built in.

Sony describe it as 'the tool of choice for media professionals who want to create and edit digital audio files with absolute speed and precision.

Acclaimed for its power, stability, and no-nonsense interface, it's the fastest way to get from raw audio to finished master. Sound Forge software is everything you need to analyse, record, and edit audio, produce music loops, digitise and clean-up old recordings, model acoustic environments, create streaming media, and master replication-ready CDs.' $300 download.

http://www.soundforge.com

### Steinberg Wavelab

Immensely capable audio editor that's always seemed a bit funkier than Sound Forge and more up with the times. Early support for VST plug-ins and other Steinberg donated goodies, easy to use, looks great. Wavelab has developed into a bit of a multitrack program which is no bad thing but does tend to blur the lines between itself and production programs like Nuendo especially with the surround sound support.

They say '1996 saw the first chapter in the long and distinguished story of WaveLab. Since then, WaveLab has been continually developed, and has become a leading application in digital audio editing. With version 5, WaveLab can once again claim to be the standard which other applications have to measure themselves by. WaveLab 5 is probably the only all-in-one solution for high resolution stereo and multi-channel audio editing, mastering, CD/DVD burning and for complete CD or DVD Audio production in outstanding audio quality.' RRP £499.

http://www.steinberg.net

## Notation software

If you head over to the websites you'll find some really good entry level versions of the notation software listed here.

### Sibelius

This has been around for donkeys, originally on the Acorn computer but in more recent years on Mac and PC. It's a truly professional score writing and composition program giving stunning layout, ease of use and amazing flexibility. It will follow your playing and adjust tempo accordingly and also allow you to type notes in from a keyboard – makes producing a score amazingly fast. The one thing that has always frustrated me is the lack of support for VST Instruments. However, Sibelius has at least made a move in the right direction providing support for a few specific software synths like its own Kompakt player with orchestral sounds and Garritan Personal Orchestra – but it's not quite far enough yet. New features though are things like support for video preview for writing to picture, which is a really bold move. RRP £595.

http://www.sibelius.com

### Coda Finale

Immensely powerful and comprehensive. No VST Instrument support but it does have Garritan's Personal Orchestra so at least it has some good inbuilt sounds (this is an optional extra with Sibelius). One of their new things is called 'Studio View' which is like a built in mixer for all the staves – looks pretty cool. Unexpected things like auto accompaniment, drum grooves and rhythm generators are all built in. Your best bet is to go along to the website and check it out for yourself. Also Coda do a range of more entry level ver-

http://www.codamusic.com

sions so if you want something simple and cheap then this is also the place to look. RRP £400.

## Software synths, instruments and samplers

This is a huge category and there's no way I could comprehensively list everything that's available. For the most up to date info check out my website http://www.pc-music.com

### Software synths

http://www.nativeinstruments.com

#### Native Instruments

Germany company with a huge software synth portfolio, for instance:

#### *Reaktor*

Now this is an incredible piece of software. It combines synthesis and sampling in a single seamless sound design package. You can patch up synths with samplers and intermingle them with effects and appegiators and filters and weird stuff. The sounds that can be created are amazing. It's much more a sound creation tool than a multi-timbral sound source although it can also be all the plug-ins you'll ever need. You can spend hours just messing with the included instruments or building your own synth – it really is that intense. Fantastic. RRP £379. Go and download the demo. Can be used as a VST Instrument or as an effect plug-in! Immense. Although not for the faint hearted.

#### *FM7*

Model of the classic Yamaha DX7 with all the FM synthesis features. It will even load old DX7 patches. In addition you get a load of effects and editing parameters not on the original. Sounds great if you want those sounds, dated if you don't. £200.

#### *Pro 53*

An accurate model of the famous old Sequential Circuits Prophet 5. A gorgeous synth that I wanted desperately as a kid and still quite fancy nowadays. This is as close as most of us will get to owning one. It sounds superb (as you'd expect from Native Instruments) and looks great although the knobs are a bit fiddly with a mouse. All controls can be mapped to a MIDI controller, which makes things simpler. Comes with stacks of great presets. Everyone should have one. RRP £149.

#### *Absynth*

Absynth is another planet of weirdness synthesis combining all sorts of different forms into what they call sound 'sculpting'. Feels very futuristic and also has a hint of wavetable like a big Korg synth. Great for rhythmic sounds and all round weirdness. £199.

# Arturia

http://www.arturia.com

French company who have managed to produce some of the most realistic models of vintage hardware synths.

### Minimoog V

Well it had to happen. People have spent so long emulating the Moog sound that it was only a matter of time before someone was allowed to use the name and be endorsed by the man Moog himself (now, sadly, no longer with us). Arturia managed it based on the quality of their sound, not to mention the fab graphics. Looks and sounds just like it should. The Minimoog is good for bass sounds, farts and squeaks.

### Moog Modular V

Moving on from the Minimoog, Arturia produced an emulation ('True Analog Emulation') of the Moog modular synth complete with patch cables and everything faithfully reproduced – 9 oscillators, 3 filter slots, 2 LFOs, 6 envelopes, VCAs, mixers, triggers, a 3x8 step sequencer. It comes with tons of presets many of which have been created by real, even famous, synth heads.

Dr Moog said: 'Arturia's Moog Modular V is a high quality computer emulation of the analog modular synthesizer that Moog Music® originally introduced... I am delighted that Arturia's Moog Modular V is adding a new dimension to an instrument tradition that has a special meaning to so many musicians.'

### CS-80V

The CS-80V is the reproduction of the legendary Yamaha® CS-80, which is considered by many as the 'ultimate polyphonic synthesizer'. Doesn't do a lot for me I have to say although at this point I am beginning to lose a little of my interest in vintage synth emulations. I'm much more into weirdness. £169.

### Arp 2600 V

The ARP2600 is one of the finest analogue synthesizers ever made and is capable of creating amazing sounds. It can be operated with or without patchcords since all of the functions are internally wired and can be controlled via sliders and switches. In addition to the original functions, MIDI control, polyphony, and the ability to create, save and recall presets are all provided. Four revolutionary tracking generators add sound design possibilities that have never been seen before. Additional effects are also provided and along with the original ARP sequencer, they form an exciting new virtual synthesizer.

# Gforce

http://www.gforcesoftware.com

Arturia may have got the endorsements but GForce and G-Media seem to have a lot more fun and manage to produce stuff that's slightly weird and off-the-wall.

### ImpOSCar

The ImpOSCar is modelled on the British '80's synth called the Oscar favoured by Ultravox, Jean Michel Jarre and Stevie Wonder, and more recently Underworld and Orbital. Download it and have a go – as the website claim that it 'Screams like a bastard' is completely true. £99.

### Oddity

The Oddity is modelled on the classic ARP Odyssey synthesiser which was manufactured between 1971 and 1976 and was used by artists as diverse as Gary Numan, Herbie Hancock, Kraftwerk and Portishead. Its place in synth folklore is assured and deserved but due to the small numbers produced, the chances of finding one in good working order for less than a king's ransom are slim. £99.

### Minimonsta

Simply put, the Minimonsta:Melohman is a Minimoog emulation on steroids. Whereas until now the numerous Minimoog clones have simply attempted to copy the original instrument and add the odd one or two features such as polyphony and another LFO, the Minimonsta takes a radically different look at an early vintage masterpiece. – they just couldn't resist doing a Moog could they. However, they have packed a load more in though. Download the demo and compare with the Arturia Minimoog V. £139.

## Spectrasonics

Sample CD company Spectrasonics came up with their own range of virtual synths using their extensive library (nice idea and essentially created the Rompler market). These are very specialist but sound amazing and, let's face it, who needs another piano sound.

### Atmosphere

The Atmosphere is a gorgeous array of pad sounds. Huge, floating, sumptuous stuff which suits me down to the ground. 3GB of samples, lots of surface editing of envelope, filters and modulation. £299.

### Trilogy

The Total Bass Module features electric, acoustic and synth bass in one handy synth. 3GB of library, 1000 sounds, these are amazing. £299.

### Stylus RMX

The original Stylus was an absolute breath of fresh looping air. Although it was just a bunch of loops stuck in an instrument the interface and way of working really made it great and intuitive to use. The RMX version builds on that and takes it to more creative heights where the original loop is just a starting point as you can go a long way from there. It has a 'Chaos' controller that messes with the loop allowing it to evolve and change constantly giving infinite variations on the sound and feel of each loop – cool. £169.

## Applied Acoustics

A slightly different form of synthesis in modelling acoustic properties and wiring them together like a synth.

http://www.applied-acoustics.com

### Tassman

A stunning acoustic modelling and synthesis program. It has the look and feel of an analogue synth but you're using mallets and plucked strings as well as oscillators. The sounds that come out of this machine are immense from the eerily lifelike to the weird and wonderful. Looks great and sounds fantastic and has a lot of the depth and complexity of Reaktor where you can mess with the synthesis engine and create your own instruments. RRP £249.

## Korg

About time one of the big hardware guns got with the program.

http://www.korg.com

### Korg Legacy

A bunch of cool software versions of old Korg gear plus a real hardware controller with knobs, patch cables and all sorts — nice idea. All sounds great especially when you layer all the synths together – amazing sounds. The controller is pretty cool but it's got mini keys and actually gets in the way a bit and makes it a bit expensive. Great synths though – The Korg Legacy Collection is the ultimate virtual instrument pack, consisting of software versions of the MS-20 and Polysix analog synthesizers, and the Wavestation advanced vector synthesizer, together with a dedicated MS-20 Controller that faithfully replicates the original MS-20 at 84% of the original size. £399. There's also a Digital upgrade to this package that includes all the sounds from the famous M1 range – awesome.

## Software instruments

Virtual versions of real instruments, or collections like those found in sound modules.

### Native Instruments

Bound to have a couple.

http://www.nativeinstruments.com

### Akoustik Piano

Akoustik Piano fuses the sampled sound, expressiveness and playability of three of the most reputable grand pianos – the Steinway D™, Bechstein D 280™ and Boesendorfer 290 Imperial™ – as well as the charismatic Steingraeber 130™ vintage upright piano into one application. Akoustik Piano covers the entire range of piano sounds and styles, transfusing the sonic characteristics and subtle tonal nuances of all four into your computer – the perfect complement for studios, rehearsal rooms, schools, stages and clubs. £199.

### Elektrik Piano

Uniting the four most beloved electric pianos of all time into one high-performance software instrument, which reproduces in exacting detail the sounds of the Fender Rhodes MK ITM and MK IITM, Hohner Clavinet E7TM, and the Wurlitzer A 200TM.

### B4 MkII

The B4 software organ broke new ground when it was released in 2000 and was an instant success. It reproduces the sound of the legendary B3 and its rotary speaker cabinet with unmatched accuracy. Its expressiveness and immediate playability continues to amaze even the most experienced organ players. The B4 II raises the bar considerably, generating a much wider sonic range and a far richer, even more authentic sound. It's an organ!

### Bandstand

Is there no end to areas that Native Instruments are prepared to cover? This is completely out of character but it's essentially a GM (General MIDI) module, like the little Microsoft built in synth, or the Quicktime one, but with 2GB of sample library making probably the most amazing sounding GM synth ever. If you are into MIDI files – playing, downloading, creating then you must get this instrument so you can experience the best sounding MIDI around. £149.

## IK Multimedia

http://www.ikmultimedia.com

Italian company who have developed some of the most comprehensive packages of sounds available.

### Sampletank 2

This is the original software sound module featuring stacks of instruments and some pretty good built in effects. Comprehensive sound collection including tons of loops and beats. Great all rounder. £199.

### Sonik Synth 2

Sonik Synth™ 2 is the ultimate synth workstation, with more synth and workstation instrument sound than any other comparable hardware or software. Over 5,000 sounds and 8.0 gigabytes make up the largest collection of modern and vintage instruments ever assembled in one product. A synth workstation on steroids. A complete songwriting, producing and arranging super tool with the widest range of high quality vintage, modern and futuristic synth and instrument sounds ever combined into one package! Basically it's Sampletank with a more synthy edge, and just as good and useful.

### Philharmonik Miroslav

Years ago a guy called Miroslav did some serious sampling of a real orchestra. It became the standard as far as sampled orchestral sounds go for Akai hardware samplers. Now IK Multimedia have taken the library and created an awesomely expressive instrument based on their Sampletank engine. It just sounds great – always has and always will. Not as huge as many orchestral libraries but it's really good. IK stick in a load of effects and stuff. £399.

# Steinberg

The creators of the industry standard Cubase VST protocol. Have their own range of software intruments.

http://www.steinberg.net

## Hypersonic

Hypersonic is Steinberg's multi-purpose music workstation that not only offers thousands of top class sounds, but is incredibly CPU and RAM efficient. Four powerful synthesis engines, 1.7 GB of top quality sounds, 1800 stunning factory presets: that's an almost overwhelming array of sounds, effects and instruments ready for use in just about any musical style or sound design application. And thanks to the unique and proprietary sample optimisation technology, each instance is exceedingly efficient with computer resources, with each instance offering up to 1024-voice polyphony across 32 stereo outputs. £249.

## Groove Agent

It's a real, pattern playing, fill triggering, style laden drum machine. Most other software 'drum machines' are really just drum sound banks, whereas this is packed with musical styles, patterns, fills, variations and a ton of drum kits. 50 odd styles to choose from and you can map styles to different kits so you can have BossaNova on a techno kit – cool. The patterns output to Cubase as MIDI so you can edit them all you want, and it's fully MIDI controllable so you can trigger changes very easily from your keyboard. It rocks. RRP £169.

## Halion Strings 2

HALion String Edition 2 features a complete string section from an orchestra in fantastic sound quality and with outstanding playability. It contains 9 GB of solo and ensemble strings recorded with one of the best European orchestras, and in combination with Steinberg's award-winning HALion 3 technology it offers different play techniques, and so is applicable for both classical arrangements and for pop/rock productions.

## Virtual Guitarist

Now this is a weird one. It's your own virtual rhythm guitarist, except this one doesn't get drunk, turn up late and try to get off with your sister. It comes packed with loads of licks and riffs, just enter the chords and off it plays, sounding a lot like a real guitar. Lots of different styles and techniques on either acoustic or electric guitar. Extraordinary. There's also an 'Electric Edition' that concentrates more on the heavier guitar riffs and also includes a nice effects rack. It certainly does what it does very well and I can see how useful it would be to people who don't play but would like to add some realistic guitar strumming into their music. RRP £149.

## Virtual Bassist

Following on to something which I think is much more useful we have a virtual bass guitarist. Using dynamic phrases based on real performances by top studio bass players in 30 styles, Virtual Bassist covers almost every conceivable music genre, delivering top class bass sounds and phrases for rock, pop, reggae, metal and hip hop to name just a few. Playing Virtual Bassist is just as easy as playing the keys on your MIDI keyboard: each style contains 2 octaves of phrases of varying complexity and fills. It's pretty brilliant really. £169.

### East West

http://www.soundonline.com

Producer of sample CDs who have grasped the whole virtual instrument idea with both hands. They have stacks of loops and instruments available as software synths and 'Romplers'.

#### *Symphonic Orchestra*

East West/Quantum Leap Platinum is the most critically acclaimed orchestral virtual instrument, with more awards than any other orchestral collection. The Platinum Edition is the top of the line. It's the only complete orchestral virtual instrument recorded in a 'state of the art' concert hall to include 3 mic positions for every sample so you can mix with real concert hall ambience. Comes as four separate instruments – Strings, Brass, Woodwind and Percussion. It does sound great. There are Gold and Silver versions as well for those who can't afford the £2000 price tag.

## Software samplers

Software designed for playing samples and sampled instruments.

#### *Native Instrument Kontakt*

This is the sampler that I use the most. The reason being for me is that it has a really easy loading interface and supports pretty much every format going. This means that as well as the great library that comes with Kontakt I can load up GigaStudio instruments, Akai instruments, Halion instruments as well as individual samples or loops. It is dead easy. It's also got some really powerful editing facilities and effects built in. It cuts the right balance of power and simplicity as far as I'm concerned and is gentler with your system than GigaStudio.

It comes with a good selection of samples from the Native Instrument range of synths as well as a special version of the massive Vienna Symphonic Library, which gives it some class orchestral sounds. £349. There's a slimline version called Kompakt for those on a tighter budget.

#### *Steinberg Halion*

Halion is a capable sampler program and without a doubt version 3 has plugged all the gaps and failings of the earlier versions. Over 50 new features in HALion 3 include 27 added effects, new sound management tools and RAMSaveT technology. The sleek new user interface and expanded routing functions add even more flexibility to the HALion experience. £249.

http://www.steinberg.net

### Tascam GigaStudio

The undisputed king of samplers is GigaStudio. No other sampler can handle the sheer volume of samples or has the quality of library available for it. Sure, other programs, like Kontakt, can load the GigaStudio library but nothing does it quite like GigaStudio does. There are so many layers built in both in samples and in functionality that it really does get into the serious realms of realistic performance. Its forte is realism, being able to produce stunningly real performances of amazingly accurate instruments. It does work best on a separate machine though – if you want to get the best out of it get a few computers and run it across the lot! I know a few people who run the Vienna Symphonic Library across 4 computers running GigaStudio, Hans Zimmer has dozens! It doesn't work as a plug-in, it runs completely independently of any other software. What it does is provide a number of virtual MIDI ports that appear in your recording software. PC only £299.

http://www.tascam.com

## Effects plug-ins

For real-time sound altering effects processing and general messing about.

### Native Instruments – Guitar Rig 2

The original was superb and included a hardware controller of four buttons and a wah pedal. It had a built in preamp and worked via control voltage rather than MIDI – a bit of a weird choice but it worked really well. Version 2 brings in a new controller that's a complete USB audio interface in itself, so you can plug in your guitar and record directly into your recording software with no other hardware required. The good bit is that you don't have to use the audio interface part of it – so if you already have an audio interface you can use them together rather than either or. The tones delivered by Guitar Rig 2's Dynamic Tube Response technology are second to none. The huge selection of equipment is astounding: Choose from 8 amps, 15 guitar and 6 bass cabinets, 4 rotary speakers, 9 microphones with adjustable positioning and 35 effects plus modulation components. Drag and drop any number of components into the virtual rack and arrange them into the desired order. A wide range of distortion, modulation, delay, reverb, pitch and volume effects allow the sound to be tuned, twisted and tweaked until the most tantalizing tones are obtained.

http://www.nativeinstruments.com

### IK Multimedia Amplitube 2

The original Amplitube took the effects market by storm and marked the reality of using a guitar with computers. They did a splendid job of producing what was essentially a software version of the Line6 Pod. However, others have caught up so it's time for IK to really deliver on this new version. There are 70 bits of emulated guitar gear allowing for over 20,000 combinations of stuff! Add in 21 stomp effects and 11 rack effects and this is one serious bit of kit. And hey, look at this, they have their own USB floorboard controller: For the first time, StompIO will offer the same feeling of working with traditional floor-processors, but with a modelling power that's unheard of. 10 foot switches, 7 knobs, 2 large displays, up to 6 configurable external controllers, MIDI

IN/OUT, hi-quality direct IN, USB , S/PDIF, balanced/unbalanced stereo OUT and more all in a rugged metal construction allow you to navigate in a traditional stomp box fashion to all of AmpliTube 2's thousands of amps and sounds. This advanced software/hardware system gives you direct access to over 4000 instantly playable presets for a monstrous sound set-up.

That sounds pretty amazing, although the difference between German (Native Instrument) and Italian (IK Multimedia) design is quite striking! The Amplitube hardware is certainly more comprehensive than the Rig Kontrol, allowing for other controllers to be connected to it and providing more controls – very interesting. £299.

http://www.amplitube.com

### Waves

One of the most respected creators of plug-ins Waves make professional, intense plug-ins for mixing and mastering. They are normally available in bundles for lots of money depending on the version but they have recently branched out into some other areas which is always good. Their Gold and Platinum bundles have been the mainstay of most software studios for many years and the new Diamond bundle takes that to another level. Their two main plugins are the L1 Ultramaximizer, a mastering limiter, and the Trueverb reverb, but they have loads these days.

http://www.waves.com

### Antares

Autotune is probably the most famous of plugins because of the scandal it seems to generate when people find out about it. Basically it's a plugin designed to correct vocal performances so you can tune flat singers and get the whole thing to sound right. It's actually very good and when used correctly should be unnoticeable (you can spot it if it's overused) and lets you correct the odd mistake that can creep into anyone's performance – nothing to be ashamed of! It no longer holds the crown it once did as there are a few other plugins that can match it's power but it's probably still the best at what it does. £239.

http://www.antarestech.com

### TC Electronic PowerCore

These plug-ins are slightly different in that they run on Powercore DSP hardware. PowerCore is a superior range of high-end plug-ins that run on tailor-made hardware. The range covers any need that you might have, and in a quality that you've probably not been used to with other VST compatible plug-ins. From basic tools like reverbs, EQs, compressor/expanders, chorus/delays, over plug-ins that are dedicated to the voice, sporting pitch correction and Voice Modelling™, to some of the very best tools on the market, like the Restoration Suite and the 'System 6000 for PowerCore' plug-ins. On top of that there are renowned synths like the V-Station from Novation and the fantastic Virus PowerCore by Access.

Undoubtedly my favourite is the Virus VSTi. I've always wanted a Virus keyboard and was never able to afford one and now I have one inside my computer – fab. They also do plug-ins from Sony and they have taken effects from their own professional hardware effects processors so you really do have the best effects available.

PowerCore Firewire – £799
PowerCore Compact – £499
PowerCore PCI MkII – £799
Optional plugins vary from about £150 to £1000.

http://www.tcelectronic.com

### Universal Audio UAD-1

The UAD-1 is a great bundle of effects covering similar ground to the PowerCore but with a more vintage edge. It's available in one of four 'PAK's' each with a different number of included plug-ins. Because of its high resolution, floating point processing, ultra high-speed memory and hardware dithering, the UAD-1 delivers outstanding high-headroom sound quality at sample rates from 44.1 to 192kHz.

Unlike other DSP cards, the UAD-1 uses a single, unpartitioned processor allowing for larger and more sophisticated plug-in algorithms offering a new level of power and complexity not found with host-based plug-ins. By greatly reducing the burden on your computer's CPU, your host application can now deliver more tracks, automation and native effects. UA uses unique proprietary circuit modelling techniques to capture every subtle nuance of analogue studio mainstays such as the 1176LN, LA-2A, Pultec EQP-1A, and Fairchild 670.

The UltraPAK has everything for £899
The StudioPAK has 20 of the good ones for £699
The ProjectPAK is a real bargain at £299 with 15 plugins
The FlexPAK is just the card with a $500 voucher to choose you own plugins from their online shop.

http://www.uaudio.com

## Hardware – soundcards

This is where you begin with the question 'What do I want to record?'. You need to match the hardware to what it is you are trying to do. Want to record a band, then look at audio cards with multiple inputs, maybe with lots of microphone preamps. Want to work purely with software synths etc? Then you just need a good quality stereo in/out card. Got loads of external synths, then get a MIDI interface with a port for each. Got a digital mixer? Then get an audio interface with the corresponding digital connections. Come on, what do you want to do?

Most soundcards you'll find for under £100 are designed for games and multimedia. They tend to lack the features us musicians are after like ASIO drivers or decent inputs, so we'll just look at those designed for music. These are usually external boxes rather than actual soundcards.

### M-Audio

These guys have been pretty prolific in terms of churning out different soundcards and audio interfaces. Recently bought by Avid, the owners of Digidesign, they've been given a special version of Pro Tools LE called 'Pro Tools M-Powered' which can run on all their soundcards. Doesn't come for free, it's about £249 extra. Here's the more interesting ones in their current

http://www.m-audio.com

range. They usually come with a pack of software like a light version of Ableton Live to get you going.

### Firewire 1814

M-Audio's flagship is the Firewire 1814 with 18 inputs and 14 outputs (the clue is always in the name) however, always be aware of how these numbers break down. It has 8 analogue inputs, S/PDIF which is digital stereo (2 channels) and ADAT light pipe, which is 8 channels of digital, giving a total of 18 inputs. It only has 4 analogue outputs, the rest being digital.

Great features are the two mic/instrument preamps, two headphone sockets, which I think is essential if you are working with other people, that can switch between two sources. £449.

### Firewire 410

Little brother of the 1814 it has only 4 analogue inputs, but 8 analogue outputs. S/PDIF gives the out two channels and it has the usual MIDI port. Two mic/instrument preamps and two headphones keep the good features present and enough outputs for surround sound mixing. £349.

### Fast Track Pro

A USB box this time, completely bus powered so no need for a power supply. Stereo analogue in/out with mic/instrument preamps and inserts for external effects, and a headphone socket. Lots of control on the front and flashing lights, this is one cool little box, perfect for getting voice and guitar into your computer with the minimum of fuss. Doesn't support Pro Tools but will run great with Cubase/Sonar etc. £199.

### Fast Track USB

A really simple USB box with mic or instrument preamp input and stereo output plus headphones. All bus powered and dead easy to plug in. Comes with some guitar effects software to get you going and for some reason this one is compatible with Pro Tools! £79.

### Ozonic

But it's a keyboard! Yes indeed but it's also an audio interface. Clever huh? So you get a 3 octave keyboard, with tons of knobs and sliders and built in stereo analogue, mic and instrument preamps, headphones, S/PDIF and MIDI in/out. What a great space saving bundle. £379.

### Audiophile

The Audiophile 2496 has been my benchmark card for as long as I can remember. If ever I'm testing out a system that doesn't seem to be working right or the soundcard isn't installing I can pop in an Audiophile and it will just work – or if it doesn't then I know there really is a problem! Great quality, great compatibility, runs ASIO, DirectX, GigaStudio, 64bit compatible and also manages most games beautifully. Simple stereo in/out, plus S/PDIF digital and a MIDI interface – perfect.

The Audiophile 192 brings support for 192kHz sampling rate making it good for high definition audio. The Audiophile 2496 is only £69 and the 192 £119 so they are real bargains for anyone who just needs high quality stereo in/out.

## Edirol

Hot on the heals of M-Audio are Edirol, a company who evolved out of Roland's desktop music division to become something fab in their own right. They seem to retain Roland's straightforwardness while giving M-Audio a run for its money in terms of features and creativity – more colourful as well. Between them M-Audio and Edirol have got the entry and mid level market pretty sewn up. So if you are looking for good solutions for under £400 then you'll probably find them here. Roland recently acquired Cakewalk so they tend to come with Sonar LE these days to get you started.

http://www.edirol.co.uk

### FA101

This nice red box offers 8 analogue in/out plus S/PDIF optical and MIDI. You've got two mic/instrument preamps and a single headphone socket. You can either run 10 outputs at 96kHz or 6 at 192kHz giving full high definition surround sound if that's interesting to you. It can be fully bus powered provided you have a 6 pin Firewire connector so for a laptop it would need a power supply (included). This is a good well behaved box with solid features. £359.

### FA66

Following the same theme the FA66 is the compact little brother of the FA101. 6 channels, 4 analogue and stereo S/PDIF plus headphone and MIDI. The obligatory twin mic/instrument preamps on the front all tied up in a nice rugged box – more rugged than most. Bus powered the same as the FA101 so laptop users will need a power supply. £279.

### UA101

Lovely metallic blue and this time one of the few USB2.0 interfaces. It's only half a rack wide but they've packed in 8 analogue in/out, mic/instrument preamps, headphones, MIDI and S/PDIF. It has a couple of nice extra features like a software mixer and router allowing you to reconnect up ins and outs internally, it's got a built in limiter for the preamps helping you to avoid distortion. £399.

## Presonus

Presonus take their gear very seriously, building preamps and compressors for professionals.

http://www.presonus.com

### Firepod

The first noticeable feature is the 8 mic preamps stuck on the front. This replaces any need for any other external gear such as mixers as you just wire the whole band straight in. And these are Presonus preamps so the quality is superb. The first two inputs and mic/instrument the rest are mic/line. You can daisy chain up another one if you like to give you 16 mic inputs – cool. The price is pretty cool too at around £500.

### Firebox

Somewhere in this little box they've packed 4 analogue inputs and 6 analogue outputs, including the twin mic preamps on the front. Also has the usual S/PDIF, MIDI and headphone socket. Can be bus powered and is made of solid metal. Even comes with Cubase LE so you have software get you going. At £249 it's cheaper than the FA66.

### Inspire 1394

It appears to be a 4 input Firewire box, with mic/instrument preamps, line and phono inputs (cool!) and stereo output. All the controls are software based and they have a really cool control panel where all the settings can be saved. But the key to this box is that they are completely stackable, up to 4 units giving you 16 inputs. The idea is that all the band members have one that they use at home, then bring along to the session and you all plug into one computer through your own interface. Nice idea, love it, will it catch on? £200.

## RME Audio

Efficient German manufacturers of no-nonsense professional gear. Little in the way of frills but lots in the way of quality and functionality. They are also ahead of the game when it comes to technology and driver writing and like to share their findings when new technology arrives or when Microsoft or Intel messes everything up again. Their range of converters and preamps is of the highest quality and so they bring a lot of technology to the table.

http://www.rme-audio.com

### Fireface 800

This is RME's way of producing a complete recording solution. Combining their own preamp and converter technology this box is actually capable of 56 channels of audio. The 10 analogue in and 8 out includes 4 mic/instrument preamps with soft limiting built in. On the back you've got 16 channels of digital ADAT and S/PDIF. That's 28 channels of input, all can be used simultaneously. You could then add another Fireface 800 or two if you like. Fabulous piece of kit if you can ever find enough things to plug into it. You get what you pay for. £899.

### HDSP9652

The best card on the market for what it does. It simply gives 24 channels of lightpipe ADAT into and out of the computer. This means you could connect up your digital mixer, like a Yamaha 02R, and run straight into the computer. Alternatively you can run the playback of something like GigaStudio straight into your digital mixer for mixing with the rest of your studio .Or you could use some really posh analogue-to-digital converters from someone like Apogee and run them straight in. Rock solid timing and sync and even a two port MIDI interface built in. £349.

## MOTU (Mark Of The Unicorn)

Although they are a Mac centred company nearly all their stuff works on PC and they work really well. A good range of boxes that really fit the bill for professional solutions. Some run on their own adapted Firewire card called the PCI424, some are just Firewire.

http://www.motu.com

### 2408MK3

The longest running MOTU box offers 8 analogue in/out plus 24 channels of ADAT and 24 channels of Tascam TDIF. It's all split into banks of 8 and you can run any three banks at once, so you could run 8 analogue, 8 ADAT and 8 TDIF, or 16 ADAT and 8 TDIF – you get the idea. A really versatile box. £749.

### 828MKII

the 828mkII provides 20 separate inputs and 22 outputs, including separate main outs and headphone out. The two mic/guitar/instrument inputs feature analogue, pre-amplified sends which allow you to insert your favourite outboard EQ, compressor, guitar amp, reverb or other effects processor before the signal goes digital. Use any input as a return. Good solid Firewire audio interface. £599.

## Line 6

Creators of the Line6 Pod guitar amp modelling effects and preamp box they have finally got around to producing a good quality recording interface for guitarists.

http://www.line6.com

### Toneport UX2

What a fab looking box, all curvy with chrome knobs and VUs, Line6 know how to appeal to the bling driven American guitarist. TonePort™ is like a rack full of premium tube recording equipment, plus a perfectly engineered recording room for guitar and bass, thanks to our acclaimed guitar/bass direct tone with mic and cab modelling. The UX2 has 2 mic inputs, 2 guitar/bass inputs, stereo line inputs, mix and monitor outputs, headphones and cool assignable VU meters on the front. You've even got footswitch jacks for start/stop control – pretty cool. It all comes with the Gearbox effects and modelling software taken from the Pod giving you a stack of great guitar tones. It's only £159.

## Digidesign

Makers of Pro Tools, the professionals choice of recording software and hardware, have a range of solutions for people who don't have ten grand to spend. Each comes with Pro Tools LE which is the 32 track version of the real thing and is pretty cool. It now supports Rewire for programs like Reason and the hardware now has ASIO drivers for Cubase etc. With their own software, as a recording solution, they are excellent.

http://www.digidesign.com

### Digi002

It's a control surface with automated faders and everything. It has up to 18 in/out (8 analogue, ADAT and S/PDIF) with 4 mic preamps, headphones and stuff. Pro Tools LE is completely controllable from the mixer. It's an ideal studio in a box sort of thing. Pro Tools LE now offers 32 audio tracks and 128 MIDI tracks, plus RTAS instruments like the Pro53 and Sampletank and Rewire which makes this a much more versatile option. Expensive though at about £1800.

### Digi002 Rack

Rack version without all the control surface bits. All the same technology and inputs and outputs in a more compact rack unit. Comes with Pro Tools LE etc. You can get them for under £800.

### Mbox 2

Basic stereo in/out with preamps, S/PDIF and MIDI and completely bus powered down USB. Very portable, £319.

## Emu

The professional wing of Creative Labs comes under the name of 'Emu' who used to make hardware samplers. They have a range of cards based upon the same technology. It's quite a complicated card as it has a DSP chip running some effects through its own mixer and so the routing between the Emu mixer and something like Cubase can get confusing, but once you know what you're doing it's really very good and the price is unbelievable (which is the positive side of being part of Creative Labs). You can also run the effects as a VST plug-in which is a nice touch. Emu have also released a software version of their hardware sampler called the EmulatorX which can only run on these cards.

http://www.emu.com

### 1820M

This combines a digital 10in 10 out ADAT and S/PDIF card with a breakout box called the AudioDock. Basically the AudioDock has got 8 analogue in/out with 2 mic preamps and a MIDI interface. Combined with the 1010 ADAT card gives you 18 in/out. The AudioDock is an annoying size and would have been so much better as a 1U rack. However, it works great and the DSP mixer and effects are useful. RRP £319. With the EmulatorX it becomes the 'EmulatorX Studio' for £399.

### 1212M

This has a stereo analogue expansion card to the 1010 ADAT card giving a total of 12 in/out. It's like having an Audiophile but with an extra 8 channel ADAT port and DSP effects for the same price of £129. Get it with the EmulatorX for £189.

# Hardware MIDI keyboards and controllers

Here are some of the best suppliers of MIDI keyboards and controllers:

http://www.m-audio.com
http://www.edirol.co.uk
http://www.behringer.com
http://www.novationmusic.com
http://www.korg.com
http://www.alesis.com

# Glossary

### ADSR
Attack, Decay, Sustain, Release, see' Envelope'

### AES/EBU
Professional format for digital transfer using XLR or Cannon connectors. Stands for Audio Engineering Society / European Broadcasting Union.

### Analogue
In electronics this describes a continuously variable signal, something which is not restricted to exact values. In music this refers to the variable electronic signal of sound going through an electrical device. Sound waves are converted into a variable electrical signal by a magnetic device like a microphone which generates electricity in response to the varying pressure of sound waves. An analogue device is also described as being linear, and as having an output proportional to its input.

### Audio
Sound waves in air, anything audible, anything you can hear. The average frequency range of human hearing is from 20Hz to 20KHz.

### Audio sequencer
A piece of software run on a computer that allows for the recording and arrangement of multiple audio tracks.

### CD quality
The quality or digital resolution at which audio CD's are recorded. 16 bit resolution, 44.1kHz sampling rate.

### Chorus
A modulation effect. Gives the impression of light vibrato or phasing, a kind of wobbly feel. Sounds nice!

### Compressor
Device used to restrict the dynamic range of a piece of audio.

### Decibel (dB)

This is a ratio and can be used to describe anything. It's often used in music to describe the difference in gain or attenuation of the amplitude of sound. E.g. boosting a signal by 6dB would mean that the signal has been boosted by a ratio of 2:1. It's a logarithmic scale and the ratio can be calculated using $dB = 20 \log x$ where $x = $ ratio.

### Delay

An effect that creates a distinct echo.

### Digital

A representation of magnitude in whole numbers or digits. Computers are digital machines. In music, recording audio digitally means that the recording is represented on a digital device by the whole values of bits (digital audio).

### Dynamic range

The difference between the quietest and loudest sound.

### Enhancer

Device used to boost higher frequencies and harmonics to produce a brighter tone.

### Envelope

How the value of a function varies with time, usually defined by 4 factors: Attack, Decay, Sustain and Release (ADSR). The most common usage is with the volume of a synthesised sound in which case the ADSR can be defined as:

- Attack – the length of time taken from when the note was struck to when the sound reaches its maximum volume
- Decay – the length of time taken for the drop of volume to occur after the sound reaches the maximum
- Sustain – the length of time the sound continues to play while the note is still held
- Release – the length of time taken for the volume to return to zero once the note has been released.

### Equalization (EQ)

Shaping the tonal character of a sound by boosting and/or attenuating certain frequencies or frequency ranges.

### Frequency

Cycles per second, measured in Hertz (Hz). How many times something happens per second.

### Full duplex

The ability of a soundcard or audio recording card installed in a computer to record and playback audio simultaneously.

### Hardware

The physical, touchable parts of a computer or other device.

### Hertz (Hz)

The unit of frequency that measures the number of cycles a waveform completes per second.

### Key mapping

Defining how the samples in a sample format file are assigned to different MIDI notes. Essentially it's the process of mapping samples across a keyboard.

### Latency

The amount of time between causing an event and that event actually happening e.g. the time between striking a key and hearing the sound of a software synth.

### MPEG

Motion Pictures Expert Group. A bunch of geezers who set up standards for multimedia.

### MIDI

Musical Instrument Digital Interface. MIDI Device Anything that responds to, or communicates with, MIDI information.

### MIDI module

A device that responds to MIDI information. Usually generates the sound of an instrument in response to a MIDI 'note on' event.

### MIDI information

A stream of instructions created by a MIDI device.

### MIDI instrument

A term used to describe an individual program or patch within a MIDI device that refers to a sound.

### Monophonic

A single tone. Used to describe a synthesiser/MIDI instrument that can only produce a single note at a time.

### MTC

MIDI Time Code. The method by which MIDI tempo, position and start/stop can be linked to SMPTE.

### Polyphonic

A synthesiser/MIDI instrument that can produce more than a single tone at a time can be described as polyphonic.

**Polyphony**

The number of tones, voices or notes a synthesiser/MIDI instrument can produce simultaneously.

**Quantization**

Moving MIDI notes (in terms of start time and length) to the nearest musical division. In other words it tidies up your sloppy timing. You can also quantize audio nowadays as well.

**Red Book**

Specifications for the production of audio compact disks.

**Reverb**

Short for reverberation, which is essentially 'echo'. When you hear an instrument being played you can also hear the echo of the instrument as the sound is reflected off walls and surfaces. Adding reverb to a recorded musical instrument gives the effect of space.

**Sample**

Digital representation of audio.

**Sampling**

The process of converting analogue audio into digital audio.

**Sampling Rate**

The number of times an analogue waveform is measured or sampled per second to convert it to digital.

**SCSI**

Small Computer System Interface.

**SMPTE**

Named after the Society of Motion Picture and Television Engineers. This is the most widely used form of synchronisation. It's a code that is recorded to tape (called striping) and contains information on position and time frame. It enables two analogue tape machines to run in perfect time with one another. Originally used to sync film and music. For us it's most useful in that SMPTE can be converted to or from MIDI time code enabling us to sync MIDI sequencers and analogue tape machines together.

**Software**

Written programs or procedures or rules and associated documentation pertaining to the operation of a computer system and that are stored in read/write memory. Okay, so it's a program usually stuck onto your hard drive.

**Sound**

See Audio.

### Synchronisation

The ability to link together two or more bits of gear so that they can share a common time reference.

### Synthesis

The artificial generation of a sound by electronic means.

### Synthesiser

A device that can synthesise sound by electronics.

### Velocity mapping

Using two or more samples, in a sample format file, on a single note each of which is triggered by a separate velocity range. So the sample used on that note changes depending on the velocity with which that note was played

### VST

Virtual Studio Technology. The audio engine created by Steinberg for their Cubase program. It sort of hangs an environment of mixing, effects and EQ over the audio output of Cubase.

### VST instrument

Software synthesiser that runs inside a VST compatible host program.

### VST plug-in

An effects plug-in compatible with the VST audio engine.

### WAV

Or wave file. The digital audio file format used by Windows.

### Wavetable Synthesis

Rather than manipulating sine waves or oscillators, wavetable synthesis uses recorded sound samples to create sounds. Synthesising musical instruments from sampled sounds requires the knowledge of which samples to store, how to store them, and most importantly, how to digitally manipulate or modulate them to produce realistic sounds. This modulation of sampled sounds is the essence of wavetable synthesis. Wavetable synthesis systems use many special techniques to create a great variety of sounds from a given amount of memory. An example is the pitch-shifting technique that can generate a number of different notes from the sample of a given instrument. For example, if the sample memory contains a sample of the middle C key on the acoustic piano, then this sample can be used to generate the C# note by shifting the pitch of the middle C upwards by one semitone. Vibrato and tremolo are effects often produced by musicians playing acoustic instruments. Vibrato is basically the low-frequency modulation of the pitch of a sound, while tremolo is the modulation of the amplitude of a sound. These effects are simulated in synthesisers by implementing low-frequency oscillators (LFOs), which modulate the pitch or amplitude of the sound produced.

## Windows

A computer operating system created by Microsoft.

## XG

Yamaha's version of the GM (General MIDI) format that includes loads of extra sounds, effects and editing.

# Contact database

**Ableton – software**
http://www.ableton.com

**Alesis – MIDI keyboards**
http://www.alesis.com

**Antares – plug-ins**
http://www.antarestech.com/

**Apple – computers**
http://www.apple.com

**Apogee – hardware**
http://www.apogeedigital.com/

**Applied Acoustics – VSTi**
http://www.applied-acoustics.com/

**Arturia – VSTi**
http://www.arturia.com

**Behringer – hardware**
http://www.behringer.com

**Cakewalk – software**
http://www.cakewalk.com

**Carillon Audio Systems – computers**
http://www.carillondirect.com

**Coda – software**
http://www.finalemusic.com

**Digidesign – hardware, software**
http://www.digidesign.com

**EastWest – software**
http://www.soundsonline.com

**Edirol – hardware**
http://www.edirol.com

**Emu – hardware, software**
http://www.emu.com

**Frontier Design – hardware**
http://www.frontierdesign.com/

**Gforce/Gmedia – VSTi**
http://www.gmediamusic.com/

**IK Multimedia – VSTi, plug-ins**
http://www.ikmultimedia.com/

**Korg – hardware, VSTi**
http://www.korg.com/

**Line6 – hardware**
http://www.line6.com

**M-Audio – hardware**
http://www.m-audio.com/

**Mackie – hardware, software**
http://www.mackie.com/

**MOTU – hardware, VSTi**
http://www.motu.com/

**Native Instruments – VSTi, plug-ins**
http://www.nativeinstruments.com

**Novation – hardware**
http://www.novationmusic.com

**Presonus – hardware**
http://www.presonus.com/

**Propellerhead – software**
http://www.propellerheads.se

**Rain Recording – computers**
http://www.rainrecording.com

**RME Audio – hardware**
http://www.rme-audio.com/

**Sibelius – software**
http://www.sibelius.com

**Sony – software**
http://www.sonymediasoftware.com/

**Spectrasonics – VSTi**
http://www.spectrasonics.net/

**Steinberg – software**
http://www.steinberg.net

**Tascam – hardware, software**
http://www.tascamgiga.com

**TC Electronic – hardware, software**
http://www.tcelectronic.com/

**Universal Audio – hardware, software**
http://www.uaudio.com/

**Waves – plug-ins**
http://www.waves.com

# Index